327.12
KIRA

WOMEN
WARTIME SPIES

2

WOMEN
WARTIME SPIES

Ann Kramer

Pen & Sword
MILITARY

First published in Great Britain in 2011
by Pen & Sword Military
an imprint of
Pen & Sword Books Ltd
47 Church Street
Barnsley
South Yorkshire
S70 2AS

ISBN 978 1 844680 58 0

A CIP catalogue record for this book is
available from the British Library.

Typeset in Palatino.

Printed in the UK by
CPI UK.

Pen & Sword Books Ltd incorporates the imprints of Pen & Sword Aviation,
Pen & Sword Family History, Pen & Sword Maritime, Pen & Sword Military,
Wharncliffe Local History, Pen & Sword Select, Pen & Sword Military Classics,
Leo Cooper, Remember When, Seaforth Publishing and Frontline Publishing.

For a complete list of Pen & Sword titles please contact
PEN & SWORD BOOKS LIMITED
47 Church Street, Barnsley, South Yorkshire, S70 2AS, England
E-mail: enquiries@pen-and-sword.co.uk
Website: www.pen-and-sword.co.uk

Contents

Acknowledgments

Thanks are due to the following:

Helen Currie for permission to quote from her experiences of working with Tunny machines at Bletchley Park.

Cynthia Waterhouse for permission to quote extracts from her private papers held in the Imperial War Museum, Documents Department.

Madeleine Brooke for permission to quote from an interview with her about her aunt, Madeleine Damerment, and for permission to photograph memorabilia belonging to her family.

The History Press for permission to quote 'The Life that I have' from *Between Silk and Cyanide*, Leo Marks, The History Press, 2009.

Random House Group for permission to quote from *Open Secret*, Stella Rimington, published by Hutchinson, 2001. Reproduced by permission of the Random House Group.

The Imperial War Museum for permission to reproduce photographs of Violette Szabo, Odette Sansom, Yvonne Cormeau and Noor Inayat Khan.

8

Timeline

1903

Erskine Chalder's *The Riddle of the Sands* is published.

1909

Britain's first Secret Service Bureau set up.

1907

First Aid Nursing Yeomanry (FANY) formed.

1911

Official Secrets Act passed, Britain.

1914-1918

First World War.

1914

4 August: First World War begins.

8 August: The Defence of the Realm Act (DORA) passed.

9 August: Aliens Restriction Act (ARA) passed.

1915

Hamil Grant publishes *Spies and Secret Service,* a history of espionage.

William Le Queux's *Spies of the Kaiser* is published; helps to stimulate spy paranoia in Britain.

September: German-born Louise 'Lizzie' Wertheim arrested, charged with spying for Germany and imprisoned.

12 October: British nurse Edith Cavell is charged with espionage and executed by firing squad in Belgium. Leads to international outrage.

1916

1 April: Belgian patriot Gabrielle Petit charged with espionage and executed, Belgium.

June: La Dame Blanche resistance and espionage network formed, Belgium and France.

1917

January: Belgian patriot Elise Grandprez charged with espionage and executed, Belgium.

July: Dutch-born Mata Hari is charged with being a German spy.

12 September: Emilie Schattermann and Leonie Rameloo shot for spying, Belgium.

15 October: Mata Hari shot by firing squad, Paris, France.

1919-38 Inter-war years

1939-45 Second World War

1939

1 September: Germany invades Poland.

3 September: Britain, the Commonwealth and France declare war on Germany.

1940

17 June: Fall of France; Pétain declares Armistice.

18 June: General de Gaulle broadcasts to France from London.

16 July: Special Operations Executive (SOE) is set up, Britain, with orders to 'set Europe ablaze'.

1941

May: Frenchman Georges Bégué is the first SOE agent to be parachuted into occupied France. In July, SOE agent Brian Stonehouse is parachuted in.

December: British government introduces conscription for women.

1942

First women SOE agents are sent into France.

24 September: Andrée Borrel and Lise de Baissac are parachuted into France.

31 October: Odette Sansom and George Starr arrive near Cannes, France, by boat.

1943

16 April: Odette Sansom and Peter Churchill arrested.

13 May: Vera Leigh and three other SOE agents arrive by Lysander near Tours, France.

16 June: Diana Rowden, Noor Inayat Khan and Cecily Lafort arrive by air near Angers, France.

20 June: Yvonne Rudellat meets SOE agents parachuted into France, all captured after skirmish with Germans.

23 June: Andrée Borrell, Francis Suttill and Gilbert Norman arrested.

15 September: Cecily Lefort arrested by Gestapo.

18 September: Yolande Beekman, and agents Harry Peulevé and Harry Despaigne arrive in France by Lysander.

13 October: Noor Inayat Khan arrested, Paris.

30 October: Vera Leigh arrested, Paris. Taken to Fresnes Prison.

18 November: Diana Rowden arrested and taken to 84 Avenue Foch. Interrogated for two weeks then taken to Fresnes.

25 November: Noor Inayat Khan, with John Starr and Leon Faye, escape but are recaptured. Noor Inayat Khan sent to Germany.

1944

13 January: Yolande Beekman (and Gustave Bieler) arrested, Paris.

28/9 February: Madeleine Damerment and two other agents parachuted into France and immediately arrested by Gestapo.

2/3 March: Eileen Nearne lands in France.

5 April: Lilian Rolfe dropped near Orléans, France.

29 April: Nancy Wake is parachuted into France.

13 May: Vera Leigh, Andrée Borrel, Odette Sansom, Diana Rowden, Yolande Beekman, Eliane Plewman and Madeleine Damerment taken from Fresnes to 84 Avenue Foch, Paris. Sonya Olschanezky joins them. All moved to Karlsruhe, Germany.

6 June: D-Day landings begin, Normandy, France.

July: Eileen Nearne arrested.

6 July: Diane Rowden, Vera Leigh, Andrée Borrel, Sonya Olschanezky taken to Natzweiler concentration camp, Alsace, France, injected with phenol and cremated. SOE agent Brian Stonehouse sees their arrival.

6 July: Christine Granville parachuted into France, joins *Jockey* network.

31 July: Lilian Rolfe arrested, taken to Fresnes prison; taken to Ravensbrück concentration camp, August.

25 August: Allies liberate Paris; de Gaulle returns; victory parade 26 August.

10 September: Yolande Beekman, Madeleine Damerment, Noor Inayat Khan and Eliane Plewman transferred to Dachau concentration camp.

13 September: Yolande Beekman, Madeleine Damerment, Noor Inayat Khan and Eliane Plewman executed Dachau.

1945

27 January: Violette Szabo shot, Ravensbrück concentration camp.

5 February: Lilian Rolfe executed and body cremated, Ravensbrück concentration camp.

8 May: V-E Day, Germany surrenders. War in Europe ends.

1946

January: Vera Atkins goes to Germany.

16 January: Noor Inayat Khan awarded Croix de Guerre posthumously.

Special Forces Club established, London, for surviving SOE members.

1948

7 May: Memorial to members of the Women's Transport Service or FANY who died during the Second World War unveiled St Paul's Church, Knightsbridge. Includes the names of women who served with SOE.

1975

Plaque put up Dachau concentration camp in memory of Noor Inayat Khan, Yolande Beekman, Eliane Plewman and Madeleine Damerment; plaque also placed in Natzweiler crematorium dedicated to '*Des quatre femmes Britanniques et Francaises parachutées exécutées dans ce camp*'.

2003

Plaque uncovered Ravensbrück concentration camp.

2011

Memorial Trust for Noor Inayat Khan raises funds for memorial statue, Gordon Square, London.

Introduction

Women of Substance

In September 2010 British newspapers and the BBC carried stories of a 'brave hero spy' who had died alone in her flat in Torquay aged 89. The woman was Eileen Nearne. She had lived the final years of her life as something of a recluse, so few of her neighbours knew anything about her or of her extraordinary past life. As details emerged it turned out that Eileen Nearne, who her niece described as a 'very private and modest person', had been one of the remarkable women recruited by the Special Operations Executive (SOE) during the Second World War. Using a false identity she had been sent into enemy-occupied France where she acted as a wireless operator for five months, sending back more than a hundred coded messages to London. Captured by the Gestapo, she was interrogated and tortured but managed to survive – and ultimately escape from Ravensbrück concentration camp. In recognition of her importance, senior military officials attended her funeral and the eulogy was given by Adrian Stones, chairman of the Special Forces Club in Knightsbridge, London, the club that was founded after the Second World War for surviving members of the SOE.

Perhaps it is not surprising that few people outside her specialist circle and immediate family knew very much about Eileen Nearne. Spying is by definition a secretive profession – a good spy passes unnoticed in a crowd – and very few women, or men for that matter, say much about what they are up to. It is also probably true to say that with some notable exceptions, most female spies or secret agents, from the courageous women of *La Dame Blanche* through to Noor Inayat Khan, have rarely received the recognition they deserve. There may be various reasons: women's achievements are often ignored, forgotten or subsumed under those of men while the nature of the work itself is a hidden one. Either way the female spies who spring to most people's minds are more likely to be women who have been immortalized through popular fiction and even legend.

Ask anyone to name a woman spy and the answer is most likely to be Mata Hari. She is probably the best known of all women spies; her exotic lifestyle, sexual behaviour and tragic death in front of a firing squad in 1917 have become the stuff of legend, and have probably coloured perceptions of women spies ever since. And yet Mata Hari was probably not a spy at all, or, if she was, she was inept and naive and quite untypical of the women who have worked in the field of espionage and intelligence gathering.

Even so, the image dies hard; only three months after Eileen Nearne was in the news, another woman made the headlines: Katia Zatuliveter, research assistant to Liberal Democrat MP Mike Hancock, who in December 2010 was alleged to be a Russian spy. Media images focused on her youth, blond hair and apparently raunchy lifestyle; she was being investigated by MI6 for possible connections to Russia's foreign intelligence service, and certainly met the received image of a 'typical' woman spy, one that has been fostered and generated through popular fiction and writers of spy history for a very long time.

It could be said that there are two major stereotypical images of women spies: the Mata Hari spy, who uses her sexuality to extract military and other secret information from unsuspecting men – a stereotype that reflects spying's tag line 'the world's second oldest profession', one assumes second only to prostitution – and who may well have been duped into espionage, perhaps by financial need or love, and the highly virtuous woman who dies heroically for love of her country. Edith Cavell, also of the First World War, is a prime example of this. She, it could be said, represents the complete reverse, all that is good in women as opposed to all that is evil. But it can also be argued that both these images were fostered for propaganda reasons, and that they reflected prevailing and deeply-held views of womanhood. Either way the images belittle women's true skills and courage in the field of espionage and certainly the reality for women who have worked as spies during wartime is quite different from the popular stereotypes.

Although often seen as a male-dominated world, which it has been until women such as Stella Rimington helped to open the doors for women, espionage – the business of obtaining secret information from an enemy, particularly during wartime – has frequently involved women. During wartime women have played very significant roles in the secret war of intelligence gathering, whether working as undercover agents in the field, listening in to enemy intelligence, decoding secret information, or as resistance fighters, harrying an enemy while at the same time obtaining crucial military information. Some of their names, particularly those of women who worked with SOE, are quite well known; others such as the women who worked with spy networks in occupied Belgium and France during the First World War have all but been forgotten.

Until about the Second World War, many male writers, such as Hamil Grant, who published a history of espionage in 1915, considered that women could never make good spies; Hamil Grant believed they were not capable of sustained patriotism, were too inclined to be knocked off course by romantic attachments and would not do the work without financial gain. On the other hand, there were those who considered that women were by nature duplicitous and therefore were to be automatically regarded with caution and suspicion during wartime in case they were spies. Other writers such as Richard Hannay or Ian Fleming continued with the stereotypes, trivializing or sexualizing the female spies in their novels, and making them subordinate to men.

But in reality women wartime spies have rarely been sexual vamps or passive dupes. There was nothing passive or subordinate about the patriotic Belgian and French women of *La Dame Blanche* who risked their lives and the lives of their families to spy on the Germans in occupied Belgium and France and send back valuable military intelligence to Britain during the First World War. Nor did they get financial gain for taking such risks. Similarly there was nothing passive, subordinate or vampish about women such as Noor Inayat Khan, Violette Szabo and Yvonne Cormeau who also risked – and in some cases lost – their lives working undercover in Nazi-occupied France during the Second World War. In both instances the women involved in undercover operations were both patriotic and extremely brave. There was opposition to using women as undercover agents during the Second World War – the dangers were enormous and, from instructors' reports during training, there were men who had serious doubts about the women's abilities and others who considered such work was not appropriate for women but eventually it was decided to use them. And, of course, women make excellent spies during wartime; on a practical level they can operate unnoticed more easily than men, they are often able to establish information networks more easily than men, and according to Selwyn Jepson, who recruited women for the SOE, women are capable of a greater and lonelier courage than men, which is certainly something women spies have frequently demonstrated. Sadly, however, many women's achievements in the field, and even their names have either been lost or ignored; only a few have won their way to some sort of fame. Most people know about Violette Szabo, heroic winner of the George Cross; far fewer know about the gentle Noor Inayat Khan who also won the George Cross, and probably even fewer about Madeleine Damerment or her French colleagues, who had previously risked their lives with the Resistance before signing up for special operations.

Operating from a safer base were hundreds of women during both world wars, who might not have risked their lives in the field but also contributed to the secret war of espionage, gathering spy catching material, coding and decoding sensitive intelligence and listening into the enemy. Their contribution to the creation and development of the British Secret Service has frequently been overlooked, particularly those who did this work during the First World War. Their achievements and dedication were remarkable but few people know their names. Those who staffed the great bombes and decoding machines during the Second World War also made an enormous contribution to the secret intelligence war, something that was recognized at the time but in this field too most of their names are unknown.

Uncovering the women who worked as spies during the First and Second World Wars, and those who worked behind the scenes during both wars, most of whose names I had not come across before has been a fascinating experience for me. Reading their files in The National Archives and tracking their achievements was enthralling. Far from being passive dupes, the women that I encountered in my research were clear-thinking, determined women who actively made their own decision to put themselves in great danger in order to fight for an ideal or patriotism or both. They also took the need for secrecy very seriously; in contrast to the received image of women as unthinking gossips, these women kept their mouths closed no matter what was done to them. They did their dangerous work, and some of them died as a result. Their names and achievements deserve to be better known than they are.

I am indebted to Tammy Proctor, whose excellent book *Female Intelligence: Women and Espionage in the First World War* first introduced me to the little-known *La Dame Blanche* intelligence gathering network about which I knew nothing at all when I started this book and which led me to Captain Landau's lively account, and also for her sharp analysis of the stereotyping and ideologically driven perceptions of women spies. I would also like to thank Madeleine (Maddy) Brooke for her time, patience and kindness in sharing information with me about her remarkable family and in particular her aunt, Madeleine Damerment, who worked with SOE and died with three other women at Dachau in 1944. I am most grateful to her as well for allowing me access to her family's papers and memorabilia; I know it is not easy for her to talk about this subject. I am grateful to Helen Currie for talking to me about her life as an ATS working on the Tunney machines at Bletchley Park and for allowing me to quote material from her personal account, and also to Cynthia Waterhouse for permission to quote extracts from her private papers which are held in the Imperial War Museum, Documents Department. Thanks also to the staff at The National Archives; the archives are a fantastic resource, it would be only too easy to disappear into them and never re-emerge; the staff are incredibly helpful. Likewise I would like to thank the staff of the Documents Department at the Imperial War Museum, who never fail to answer questions and provide help. And finally my thanks to St Paul's Church, Knightsbridge, for providing me with photographs of the WTS Memorial and to Simon Adams who clambered onto his bicycle and braved a rainy day to take photographs of the Violette Szabo mural and blue plaque in Stockwell. I am most grateful.

Chapter 1

Women and War

'Upon women the burden and horrors of war are heaviest.'
Margaret Sanger

War impacts profoundly on women's lives, whether on the home front, in occupied territories, or on the battlefield. With the advent of total war and the mass mobilization of civilian populations during the twentieth century, women's formal involvement in war increased enormously. The two World Wars had an impact on women's lives that was far greater than in previous wars, not least because aerial bombardment, invading armies and the enlistment of whole populations brought war directly into the home, affecting civilians on the home front – a term that was coined during the First World War – just as much as soldiers on the frontline. During both World Wars women were involved in myriad roles: maintaining homes and families, doing war work, in caring roles as nurses and doctors, working within the armed forces – and as information gatherers, spies and resistance fighters. Many, although not all, were roles previously only held by men, or believed to be suitable only for men.

Opening the Doll's House: women's war work
Writing in 1917 about women's involvement in the war, American journalist and feminist Mabel Potter Daggett declared: 'I think we may write it down in history that on 4 August 1914, the door of the Doll's House opened... For the shot that was fired in Serbia summoned men to their most ancient occupation – and women to every other'. To some extent she was correct; between 1914-1918 and even more so between 1939-1945, the demands of war meant that women were pulled out of their more traditional roles as homemakers and carers and plunged into activities previously dominated by men.

In Britain, when the First World War broke out, large numbers of women, including several who had spent the pre-war years fighting the British government for the right to vote, now demanded the right to be involved in the war effort. Leading suffragist, Millicent Fawcett writing in *The Common Cause* urged: 'Women your country needs you... let us show ourselves worthy of citizenship whether our claim to it be recognized or not.' Emmeline Pankhurst too, charismatic leader of the militant Women's Social and Political Union (WSPU), called an end to suffragette activities and threw her influence behind the British government, actively helping to recruit men – she and her supporters were reputedly involved with the appalling white feather movement – and urging the government to use women in the war effort. These calls on women to back the government split the women's movement but even so as increasing numbers of men were left to die in the trenches, an estimated two million women entered the labour force, working for the first time as bus and tram drivers, painters and decorators, postal workers, bank clerks, butchers and munition workers producing thousands of shells while their faces and hair turned yellow from the DDT. Women worked as chimney sweeps, delivered milk, toiled on the land in the newly-formed Women's Land Army and were employed as communication workers and police. By the end of the First World War, women in Britain and some of the other warring countries were doing just about every job imaginable to help the war effort – and this at a time when, with the exception of Australia and New Zealand, women did not have the vote, nor did many people believe they should have. Their involvement in war work did not necessarily open the doll's house but despite considerable male prejudice it challenged the conventional view that a woman's place was only in the home, so much so that in January 1919 *The Times* featured an article about a forthcoming exhibition on women's wartime work to be held at the Imperial War Museum, which would inform the public of the 'extraordinary range and variety' of the work that women had done on the home front and in military hospitals.

The guns of the First World War fell silent on 11 November 1918 and as surviving soldiers returned from fighting, women were encouraged to give up the waged work they had done during the war, and return to their domestic roles. Most did so, some with relief, but nothing was ever quite the same again. During the inter-war years women in Britain, the United States and various other countries finally gained the vote. More women enrolled in universities and an increasing number of occupations began to open up for women. The First World War had also left a specific legacy: many women had lost husbands and fiancés, leaving a considerable number of single women, many of whom forged independent lives. From the mid-1930s however worldwide economic depression, coupled with the rise of Fascism in Italy and Nazism in Germany were ominous signs, and as the decade wore on it appeared that a second major conflict was emerging. In Britain, from 1938, the government began to make plans to put the country onto a war footing.

To some extent women's involvement in war work during the First World War was voluntary, fed by a wave of patriotism and government propaganda as well as by the need for women to replace the men who had gone to fight. During the Second World War Britain organized for 'total war' and government recruitment drives for women workers were even more intense, with propaganda and radio broadcasts urging women to come into the factories and 'do their bit'. From spring 1941 every woman in Britain aged between 18-60 had to register with employment exchanges and those who were suitable had to choose from a range of possible wartime occupations. So urgent was the need for women to be involved in the war effort that in December 1941, under the National Services Act (2), the British government took the unprecedented step of introducing conscription for single women aged 20-30, although it was emphasized that women would not be required to bear arms. By the end of the war the total number of British women in war work was around 7,750,000, two million more than in 1939. Once again, women did every job imaginable, working on the railways, in shipyards, in transport and factories. Some 80,000 women also worked on the land in the Women's Land Army and Women's Timber Corps, helping to bring in 70 per cent of the nation's food by June 1943. Women worked as engineers, welders, carpenters and electricians; they built roads and barrage balloons; drove tractors and farmed the land; and helped to produce millions of tons of armaments but, despite doing the same work as their male counterparts, women consistently received less pay.

Women's entry into male-defined areas of work, whether agriculture or industry, did not go without comment and during both wars women workers faced considerable opposition and discrimination not least from male trade unions, who feared that the employment of women would jeopardize male status and wages. During the First World War women workers were frequently lampooned in magazines such as *Punch* and there were considerable fears that involvement in work considered to be more suitable for men would harm a woman's frail femininity at best, and undermine her morals at worst. There were considerable debates within the press and parliament about women's work, particularly the use of married women; during the Second World War for instance, wartime Prime

Minister Winston Churchill expressed his concern that women's involvement in factory production would seriously damage family life. Even so, by 1943 in Britain, nine out of ten single women and eight out of ten married women were officially involved in the war effort, whether on the land, in war industries or in the armed forces.

Forces women

From 1917 British and American women were also enlisted into the armed forces to free up more men for combat. In Britain the Women's Army Auxiliary Corps (WAAC) and the Women's Royal Naval Service (WRNS) were set up in 1917; one year later the Women's Royal Air Force (WRAF) was also formed. Women wore uniform and learned to drill and take orders but then, as now, were not allowed to fight. Instead they provided a host of support duties, such as clerical and catering work. They worked as telephone operators and also worked in signals intelligence, listening into and passing on messages, some of them intercepted from enemy sources.

When war broke out again in 1939, women in Britain flocked to join the Auxiliary Territorial Service (ATS), the women's section of the army, the Women's Royal Naval Service (WRNS), or the Women's Auxiliary Air Force (WAAF). There was also the Women's Transport Service (WTS). By 1943 more than 500,000 women were serving in the ATS, WRNS and WAAF combined. In the United States women served in the Women's Army Corps (WAC) and were sent to all theatres of war. Once again, women in the auxiliary services were not allowed to engage in combat but they worked as drivers, cooks and clerks, freeing men to go and fight. As war progressed, however, forces women worked in command centres and operation rooms as telephone operators or using radar and radio to plot ships and planes. There might have been a veto on women picking up arms but women worked alongside men on the anti-aircraft guns; they may not have been allowed to fire the guns but this was a moot point, they certainly pinpointed the targets.

Women on the front line

It is often assumed that women do not engage in combat and certainly in Britain and the United States, to this day, women in the armed forces are forbidden to pick up arms. However, the reality for many women during times of war has been quite different. Throughout history there have been warrior queens, such as Boudicca, while individual women have also defied convention to fight alongside men on the front line. One notable example during the First World War was Englishwoman Flora Sandes, who fought with the Serbian Army and eventually gained the rank of captain. During the First World War Russian women fought on the frontline in the so-called Battalion of Death; led by Maria Botchkareva a battalion of some 300 Russian women fought at the front side by side with men; they suffered heavy casualties. During the Second World War Soviet women pilots, known as the 'Night Witches', carried out more than 23,000 night bombing raids over German territory, targeting railways, ammunition dumps and artillery positions. In occupied territories too, where women are particularly vulnerable to deprivation and abuse, women have picked up arms to defend themselves and their families and have joined resistance movements, harrying and killing the enemy. The view of women as non-combatants therefore is not strictly accurate.

During both World Wars women made their way to the front line as nurses, doctors, ambulance drivers and cooks. Nursing and caring for the wounded to some extent falls into an area of work traditionally seen as female-appropriate but the work of pioneer Florence Nightingale during the Crimean War legitimized the idea that women could work near the front line. For the public, particularly during the First World War, wartime nurses were often seen as angelic beings, mopping fevered brows but as always the reality of wartime nursing was not that simple: women, many of them from sheltered privileged homes, came face to face with horrendous wounds and appalling conditions, working with scarce resources, often under fire, in makeshift field hospitals, not far from the front line. The rules of war stated that women were not supposed to nurse on the battlefield but in practice many did, including the daring Elsie Knocker and Marie Chisholm who set up a first-aid post at Pervyse, Belgium, right on the front line, gaining the British Military Medal for rescuing a British pilot from no-man's land. Women such as the Scotswoman Dr Elsie Inglis, whose offer of help was turned down by the British War Office – they told her to 'go home and sit still' – funded her own hospitals in France, Romania and Serbia during the First World War. And twenty years later, thousands of women continued the tradition working as nurses and doctors in Britain and in war zones abroad, where they worked in makeshift field hospitals as near to the front line as possible, often under heavy bombardment.

One uniformed unit that became very well known during the First World War was the First Aid Nursing Yeomanry (FANY). First formed in 1907, and consisting largely of highly privileged and rather dashing women, the FANYs (as they became known) drove ambulances in France and Britain, and became renowned for their daring exploits. Later, in the Second World War, they were a recruiting source for British intelligence and special operations.

Spying and intelligence

Wars are not only fought in the open, they are also fought in secret as governments and armed forces attempt to find out what their enemy is planning. Espionage and intelligence gathering are an integral part of all wars but not visible to the general public. By and large this has often been seen as 'men's work' but women too have played a major role. During both World Wars women were highly visible in food queues struggling to maintain their families and homes, as volunteer or civil defence workers, in wartime factories and as members of the auxiliary armed forces. But one of the rolls which were taken on by women during wartime was far less visible and less well known – that of intelligence gathering and espionage.

During the First World War a large number of courageous women, whose names are virtually unknown today, worked as spies for British intelligence in enemy-occupied territories

'In times of war and peace governments will always seek other countries' information to give them an advantage in international situations.'

(Stella Rimington)

obtaining and passing back valuable information that was then used to plan combat strategies. Women in Britain also worked in the newly formed British Secret Service, listening into enemy signals, helping to code and decode messages, and keeping details on suspected enemy spies and espionage activity in Britain. As Tammy Proctor has described in her excellent book *Female Intelligence: Women and Espionage in the First World War*, it is only very recently that their contribution has begun to be recognized. Twenty years later even more women worked in British intelligence, while others were specially trained and equipped to spy and work with resistance movements behind enemy lines, adopting false identities and risking death. While some of the women who spied during the Second World War have become fairly well known, those who worked in intelligence and espionage during the First World War are almost entirely unknown, with some notable exceptions. Obviously by its very nature espionage is a secretive profession and many women did not talk about their work once war was over. However, their invisibility may also indicate that women spies and intelligence workers, particularly during the First World War, have been overlooked or even trivialized because until recently their efforts and contribution have not been taken as seriously as those of men. It might also suggest that the use of women in these covert areas has also been regarded as somehow inappropriate.

There is nothing new about women working as spies, although the historical examples that are given, particularly by male writers, do tend to stress women's sexuality as being the prime requisite for the task. Since Biblical times women have worked as spies – Delilah being considered by many historians to have been the earliest recorded example. More recently during the American Civil War, for instance, a number of women such as Belle Boyd and Harriet Tubman worked as spies. Belle Boyd spied for the Confederate side, operating from her father's house and passing on information to Confederate generals. She was eventually betrayed and arrested. Harriet Tubman, the black American abolitionist who ran the so-called Underground Railroad, worked for the Union side, scouting in enemy territory and bringing back important military intelligence. Also during the seventeenth century, the writer Aphra Behn worked as a spy for the British government, although the information she obtained was disregarded.

Over the following two centuries, a number of other significant women, including Gertrude Bell, were engaged in gathering sensitive information for Britain. Gertrude Bell was in fact the first woman formally employed by British intelligence as a political officer. Born in 1868, she studied history at Oxford University and gained first-class honours, although that university did not actually award degrees to women until 1920. She went on to become one of the great Victorian women travellers, spending a great deal of time in the Middle East. She provided maps and other information to British intelligence about the Middle East and, given the political tensions of the time, her information was gratefully received. In 1916 she was formally employed by the Arab Bureau.

'Being a spy in wartime means real hard, risky work. One is engaged in the "Secret Service", one is always working in the dark, and one is liable at any moment to be trapped – to meet death secretly and mysteriously, or to face a firing-squad.'

(Marthe Richer)

Spying is a risky business: whether male or female, someone who adopts a false identity to obtain information from within an enemy's territory is usually risking death, something that Marthe Richer, a First World War spy, made a point of emphasizing in her book *I Spied for France*. It is often said that women make very good spies, particularly during wartime because they can pass unnoticed where a man, whether in uniform or not, is more likely to arouse suspicion. Also women have neighbourhood networks,

Aphra Behn 1640-1689

USUALLY CONSIDERED TO be one of the first English women to earn her living as a writer, Aphra Behn was also a spy but perhaps because she was a woman, the valuable information she acquired was disregarded. There is some debate about the details of her life but Aphra Behn was probably born in Wye, near Canterbury. Her mother, Elizabeth Denham, was a nurse to the wealthy and influential Culpepper family who, in around 1663, visited Surinam taking Aphra with them. Returning to England in 1664, Aphra met and married Johan Behn, a merchant of Dutch or German extraction. There is disagreement as to whether the two actually married but either way, Johan died soon afterwards. Having become part of the royal circle through her Culpepper connections, Aphra Behn was recruited as a spy in 1666. The Second Anglo-Dutch War had broken out the previous year and, using the code name Astrea, a name she later used for her published writings, Aphra Behn, who spoke Dutch fluently, was sent to Antwerp to obtain information about the Dutch military capabilities and political intentions towards Britain. This Aphra Behn did, sending back coded information that the Dutch Admiral de Ruyter planned to launch fire ships against the British fleet. For whatever reason – some have said because she was a woman – Aphra Behn's information was ignored or dismissed. The Dutch fleet did indeed sail up the Thames and torched British man-of-wars in the Thames. To add insult to injury, Aphra Behn was blamed for this, and never paid for her work. Espionage's loss was literature's gain. Following this experience, Aphra Behn turned to writing to earn a living, producing some of the most important women's writing of the seventeenth century. She died in 1689 and is buried in Poet's Corner, Westminster Abbey.

which provide useful channels for passing information, sometimes denigrated as 'gossip' but they still remain just as vulnerable as men. In Britain, the use of women for intelligence gathering work was fairly random until the twentieth century, operating informally and within environments such as diplomatic circles. This changed in the early part of the twentieth century with the establishment of Britain's first Secret Service in 1909 and the coming of the First World War meant the need to obtain good intelligence was crucial and the process was put onto a far more organized and professional footing.

Chapter 2

Spy Paranoia and the First World War

'Beware of Female Spies. Women are being recruited by the enemy to secure information from Navy men, on the theory that they are less liable to be suspected than male spies. Beware of inquisitive women as well as spying men.'

WORLD WAR I POSTER

In March 1909 a sub-committee of Britain's Committee of Imperial Defence, the government body that had been established in 1904 to organize Britain's defence and military preparations, met to discuss the question of foreign spies in Britain, most particularly the threat to British naval ports from German spies. Seven months later, in October 1909, Britain's first Secret Service Bureau was established. Consisting initially of a small staff, and headed by Captain Vernon G.W. Kell of the South Staffordshire Regiment and Captain Mansfield Cumming of the Royal Navy, the new Bureau's task was to co-ordinate intelligence work, and in particular to explore the threat posed by German spies. Working on behalf of the War Office and the Admiralty, the two men worked together initially but after a while it became clear that the task was two-pronged: to investigate what was going on in Britain and stop it, and to send agents into Germany to find out what was going on there. As a result, by 1910 the Bureau had divided into two sections, one headed by Kell that was responsible for counter-espionage, investigating and catching foreign spies in Britain, and the other, headed by Cumming, who became known as 'C', which was responsible for gathering information abroad. The first eventually became MI5 and the second became MI6.

Spy paranoia
The new Secret Service Bureau came into being at a time of intense

spy paranoia. The years leading up to the First World War saw an increasing rivalry and escalating arms race between Britain and Germany that found expression in a growing anxiety about the presence of German spies in Britain and the possibility of a German invasion. British newspapers printed sensational accounts of German spies living and working in Britain, which were fuelled by an outpouring of colourful pre-war spy literature and novels that either depicted German plans to invade Britain or presented the existence of an established German intelligence network. One of the earliest was *The Battle of Dorking* (1871), a short story by George Tomkyns Chesney, which described the invasion of England by Germans. Another very influential novel was *The Riddle of the Sands* (1903) by Erskine Childers. Often considered to be the first true spy novel, it featured two patriotic young men – Davies and Carruthers – who, sailing around the tidal waters and sandbanks of the German Frisian islands, uncover a German plan to invade England.

The most prolific spy writer however was the Anglo-French journalist William Le Queux, whose best-known works included *The Invasion of 1910* (1906), which was initially serialized in the *Daily Mail* and then subsequently published as a novel, selling over a million copies. Presenting himself as involved in counter-espionage work, Le Queux went on to publish *Spies of the Kaiser: Plotting the Downfall of England* (1915), which, although described as a novel, he claimed was the result of 12 months travelling around Britain during which time he claimed to have uncovered the presence of 5,000 German spies. His claims were massively exaggerated: the German navy did employ a small number of spies before the war but not nearly as many as Le Queux claimed. Between August 1911 and July 1914 only ten suspects were actually arrested by the War Office's counter-espionage department. Even so writings such as those of Le Queux had an enormous impact, stimulating the establishment of the British Secret Service, and helping to promote spy fever and the anti-German feeling which swept the country before the war.

Once war began in 1914 spy mania intensified in Britain, fostering widespread anti-German feeling and xenophobia. In Britain the Aliens Act of 1905 had begun to limit immigration and in 1911 the Official Secrets Act was passed, which gave intelligence services extraordinary powers to investigate and prosecute anyone suspected of espionage, and anyone suspected of harbouring a spy. The Defence of the Realm Act (DORA) was passed in 1914 for securing public safety and extended the 1911 Official Secrets Act to give the British government sweeping powers to requisition property, control labour, apply censorship and to move not just against spies and traitors but also anyone suspected of speaking against the government or British war aims. A day later the Aliens Restriction Act (ARA) was passed, which extended the State's right to monitor and control foreigners in Britain, imposing permits and no-go areas for aliens. All aliens had to register with their local police. By 9 September 1914 more than 50,000 Germans and some 16,000 Austro-Hungarians had registered; thousands of them would be interned during the war.

Nicholas Everitt, who worked with the British Secret Service during the First World War, claimed there were more than 14,000 German, Austrian and 'foreign' spies actively at work in Britain at the outbreak of war. Given their new and draconian powers, police and security services moved against suspected spies with impunity, and there were constant references in the British newspapers to German spies, or suspected spies being discovered, investigated, rounded up and imprisoned. On 6 August 1914, for instance, under a dramatic headline 'The Danger From Spies', *The Times* reported that during the preceding 24 hours, some twenty-one spies had been arrested 'chiefly in important naval centres'. The article also referred to another dozen arrests that had taken place in London, one of those arrested including an 'alleged spy who was staying at a fashionable hotel in the vicinity of Hyde Park'. Numerous similar reports of arrests and investigations followed on an almost daily basis. On 11 August 1914 *The Times* reported that 'several cases of espionage or attempted outrage by supposed spies' had been reported from various parts of Britain, including Aldershot where a military picket had arrested two men cutting telephone wires, Dunoon where a woman suspected of being a German spy had been arrested at the Millhouse gunpowder works, and at Nottingham, where one Max Kuhner, formerly of the German Army, had been remanded 'on the charge of obtaining information calculated to be to be useful to the enemy.' Apparently plans of Nottingham, Brussels and places in Germany had been found in his lodgings, together with a loaded revolver.

The frenzy did not stop at suspected spies: as time passed paranoia extended to all foreigners living in Britain, but particularly Germans, who were usually described as enemy aliens. Despite on the one hand suggesting that the public should not regard all foreigners as spies, the public were nevertheless urged to be on their guard and to report anything suspicious to the authorities, so effectively whipping up anti-German feeling. On 25 August 1914, while announcing new measures to be introduced for 'stamping out spying and sabotage by alien enemies', *The Times* reminded its readers that there were at that time 50,000 'alien enemies, subjects of the German and Australian Empires' in the United Kingdom and went on to say that thousands of 'resident Germans – waiters, barbers and the like' had lost their jobs since the war began and that 'the adage concerning work for idle hands naturally occurs to the mind' going on to describe many of the resident Germans as 'suspicious characters' and to make the point that while the 'danger is not one to cause a panic… it should certainly not be underestimated…', an approach unlikely to calm the public's nerves. Merely a day later, on 26 August, *The Times* commented that the 'spy danger… is still with us…. The duty of the public is a simple one. It is to report to the police whenever they think there is justification for such a step'. The following day *The Times* stated that 'while it is unnecessary and foolish to assume that every German in this country is a spy, it should be remembered that the Germans have probably the most complete espionage system of all the European Powers and we may assume that our own country has received the attention of not the least able of the German emissaries'.

Given such an approach it is hardly surprising that rumours and false stories about spies were rife; foreigners, even long-term residents, were automatically regarded with suspicion, as was virtually anyone who was considered to be behaving oddly. It was no time to be German or to seem in any way foreign. Anonymous letters poured into police offices drawing attention to anyone who was acting suspiciously and making wild accusations. Not surprisingly there were many false arrests, including the Mayor of Deal who was arrested on Dover cliffs on suspicion of espionage and taken under armed guard in front of the military authorities. In an attempt to reduce any communication channels that might be used by potential spies, people who kept homing pigeons were also rounded up. More significantly though, the government used its sweeping powers to round up hundreds of foreigners, either deporting them or interning them for the duration of the war.

Spy frenzy was not confined to Britain; it also raged through Northern France, Belgium and Germany. Refugees were rounded up, there were reports of German soldiers in plain clothes or French uniforms signalling to their troops with coloured lights at night and puffs of smoke during the day, and it was believed that thousands of people around Antwerp were spying for Germany. Unwary British travellers in Germany also found themselves being detained as suspected spies, something of course that the British press reported with horror and outrage: it was perfectly acceptable to round up foreigners in England but quite unacceptable for British travellers to be inconvenienced.

According to police records, spies could be found in a wide variety of occupations and activities. No one was above suspicion. On 26 August 1914, *The Times* published the list of the occupations of foreigners recently arrested on charges of espionage. The list included: 'Hairdressers (3), German naval pensioner, bookkeeper, music-hall artist, German consul, engineer, waiter, pastor of German seamen's museum, subaltern, student, cook, mariner, cabinet-maker, photographer, director of margarine works, director of oil company, professor of languages, and ship's chandler.' Other occupations also regarded as suspect were foreign governesses and domestic servants.

During the course of the war thousands of aliens were interned or deported. On 2 September 1915 within an article entitled 'The Alien Enemy', *The Times* reported that 500 Germans and Austrians – 'alien enemies' – had been interned during the previous five or six days. The article went on to state that the methods adopted by German spies to obtain and send information showed 'considerable ingenuity' and including tapping telephone wires and using pigeon post. Interestingly, the article also stated that 'Women as well as men are engaged in the work [of spying]. Recently a German governess in a London family departed, leaving some of her possessions behind. The house was visited by the police, who found among some papers in a locked trunk careful and detailed sketches of railway bridges and their environs.'

Images of women spies

By and large spying was considered to be a distasteful profession. Winston Churchill, for instance, in his foreword to *I Was a Spy!* by Marthe McKenna, who spied for the British Secret Service during the First World War, described it as a 'terrible profession', and certainly spies, particularly those spying for the enemy, were seen as people of low moral fibre and 'degenerates'.

Female spies were seen as particularly distasteful and dangerous, reflecting some of the prevailing views of women at that time and the concern was that their very existence damaged the moral fibre of a nation. Fictional images of women spies ranged from sexually depraved individuals of the *demi-monde* who lured their prey into revealing state secrets, or as helpless dupes, conned into espionage by love of another – male – spy. Either way, intelligence officers had an ambivalent and sometimes contradictory view of women spies. It was generally believed that women had an advantage in that they could blend into the background and, if employed as governesses or maids, could have access to information which would be useful to the enemy. At the same time, most intelligence officers considered that in the end women could never make good spies because their emotions ruled their behaviour; they were too likely to fall in love and hence to jeopardize their work. It was also considered that women became spies for base motives: they were not capable of being patriotic, in the same way as men.

In his book *Spies and Secret Service*, a history of espionage which was published in 1915, Hamil Grant stated clearly that 'Women… are rarely effective or satisfactory agents in secret service'. In his view it was not because women were incapable of 'sounding lower depths than the vilest of the male species', but that 'they are rarely to be relied upon once romantic sentiment becomes engaged in their operations.' Going further, Grant claimed that 'it is extremely rare that women display either the self-restraint or the reasoning power… in matters of love or revenge, where her deepest feelings are concerned, she is capable of a sustained effort calling for the application of whatever analytical powers she may possess, but seldom in other cases; for an appeal to, say, her patriotism leaves her almost invariably cold and unenthusiastic, since love of country is a quality which depends too largely on an essentially platonic and impersonal principle to attract and hold for long her undivided attention.' In other words, women spies, like all women in Grant's opinion, were incapable of being subjective, analytical or patriotic.

Hamil Grant was not alone in his views. French intelligence officer Ferdinand Tuohy, writing in the 1920s, also considered that women made poor spies because of their tendency to fall in love. By the 1930s he was revising his views slightly, although he obviously felt that women's role was that of auxiliary to male agents. Writing an article on spies for the *Daily Mail* in 1937 he clearly stated that going after the 'real secrets' such as blueprints was strictly a man's job, but that it was 'idle to pooh-pooh the potential value of women agents', particularly during peace time, when as secretaries they are in a good position to steal and copy documents.

When war began the newly formed Secret Service under Kell had a list of suspected spies, who were immediately watched or detained. There were a few women on the list although by 1916 only just over 240 women were being watched, had been detained or were banned from military zones, compared with well over 1,000 men. Just about every woman of German or Austro-Hungarian origin came under surveillance, even if they had become British citizens by marriage. Most of those arrested and charged were caught as a result of letters being opened, or tip-offs by neighbours, or by association with men already under surveillance. But very few of the women spies captured in Britain came anywhere near the fictional images of women spies. They included Martha Earle, a German-born 64-year-old woman who had obtained British citizenship when she married a British headmaster in 1908. The letters she wrote to her sister in Germany were intercepted and she was arrested and sentenced to one year's imprisonment in Holloway for sending coded information in her letters. Earle claimed she had used a family code and that she had only written to her sister. The information she sent had no military value but nevertheless, whether Earle's actions can be seen as spying or not, Earle was considered to have committed a crime and was convicted.

Another German-born woman charged and imprisoned for espionage was Louise 'Lizzie' Wertheim, who had arrived in England in 1902 and married a naturalized British citizen. They separated in 1913. She subsequently met George T. Breeckow, a German spy living in London under the assumed name Reginald Rowland, they became romantically involved and worked together. Wertheim's hotel room was searched and substances found that could be used for invisible ink. Breeckow and Wertheim were arrested and tried in September 1915. Breeckow took sole responsibility and was executed, death being the penalty for espionage. Wertheim was sentenced to ten years' imprisonment in Aylesbury Prison, where conditions were particularly harsh. The British authorities had by this time, and particularly following the British outrage following execution of Edith Cavell by the Germans, decided not to execute women spies caught in Britain. Wertheim died of natural causes in prison in Aylesbury Prison in 1921.

A handful of other German-born women arrested for espionage during the war included Martha Earle's daughter, Eleanor Polkinghorne, Louise von Zastrow Smith, Lina Heine, Heddy Glauer and Marie Kronauer. Also arrested for espionage were Danish-born Eva de Bournonville, and French-born Albertine Stanaway. Many went to prison protesting their innocence or claiming that information they had sent was of little importance. Some protested the harsh conditions in prison and most were deported in 1918. In the end, despite the thousands of names that were gathered by intelligence officers and police, only thirty German spies were finally arrested in Britain between 1914 and

1918. Twelve, all men, were executed, one committed suicide and the others were imprisoned.

Virtuous nurses and exotic dancers: the archetypes

Two of the best-known women spies of the First World War – in fact two of the best-known women of the First World War – were Edith Cavell and Mata Hari. The two women could have not have been more different and, strictly speaking, neither of them was actually a spy or, in the case of Mata Hari, not a very successful one. Both women were executed but the way in which they were portrayed and the reaction to their deaths varied enormously: Edith Cavell was seen as a virtuous and humanitarian martyr, who died for her country, Mata Hari as an exotic, dangerous, self-interested and vamp-like female spy. Both images reveal much about how women were perceived at the time and both provide clues to the enduring myths and stereotypes about women spies that continue to this day.

Edith Cavell was a nurse; an occupation that was seen during the First World War as an honourable and virtuous activity for women. She was born on 4 December 1865 in the village of Swardeston near Norwich into a middle-class family; her father was the local vicar. She was well-educated and initially worked as a governess but subsequently took up nursing as a career, working in Manchester. In 1907, aged in her early forties, she went to Belgium where she was invited to head a pioneer training school for nurses, a task that she fulfilled efficiently, introducing strict regimes and expanding the potential of the nursing school. In a letter home, Edith Cavell wrote that there was still prejudice in Belgium against women taking waged work, but after the Queen of Belgium used one of the trained nurses from the school to treat a broken arm, the school's status was assured and by 1912 the training school was providing nurses for various hospitals, schools and kindergartens.

When war began in 1914, Cavell remained in Belgium. The training school became a Red Cross Hospital, treating both Belgian and German wounded. The British retreat from Mons in September 1914 and German advances into occupied Belgium had left French, British and Belgian soldiers stranded behind enemy lines. In November 1914 two stranded British soldiers, separated from their units, found their way to the hospital where Cavell hid them for two weeks before helping them to escape to neutral territory in Holland. Over the next few months Cavell continued to hide refugee soldiers when they arrived at the hospital; she also helped them with new identities and found couriers to help them to escape occupied Belgium, many of them to rejoin the Allied forces. From February 1915 Cavell and her hospital became the hub of a much larger underground escape network that involved 'guides' who moved men from one safe house to another and so-called 'chemists', who produced forced identity papers. The network itself was based near Lille in Northern France and Mons in Belgium; soldiers arrived at Cavell's hospital and were then moved along the network from occupied Belgium into the Netherlands. Various other women were also involved including Belgian aristocrat Princess Marie de Croÿ, whose surname backwards – Yorc – was used as a password, a French teacher Louise Thuliez, and Comtesse Jeanne de Belleville. De Croÿ and her brother Reginald hid soldiers in their chateau in Mons, as did de Belleville at her home in Montigny-sur-Roc. Thuliez either escorted soldiers to hideouts or took them to Cavell in Brussels, where they were hidden and nursed while Cavell made escape arrangements. Guides were organized by Philippe Baucq, an architect, who also helped to plan escape routes, while Hermann Capiau, an engineer, was one of the guides, often taking soldiers to Cavell's school. Exact figures are not known but at least 200 Allied soldiers were helped to escape from occupied Belgium.

By summer 1915 the Germans were beginning to get suspicious and searched Cavell's school in June but found nothing incriminating. Apparently Cavell remained perfectly calm while the search was taking place. On 31 July 1915 however two members of the escape team – Thuliez and Baucq – were arrested with evidence of their escape activities. Five days later on 5 August Cavell was also arrested and taken to St Gilles Prison. Subsequently another thirty-five members of the network were also arrested. During questioning Cavell confessed almost immediately to her involvement in the network and openly admitted both then, and later at her trial, that she had helped to nurse, hide and help Allied soldiers to escape from Belgium to rejoin their army, even though she would have known that this was a capital offence under German law.

Cavell and the other prisoners were tried in Brussels between 7-11 October 1915. Twenty-six of the accused were found guilty of treason and five were sentenced to death, one of whom was Edith Cavell. Early the following morning, despite intervention by neutral American and Spanish embassies, Edith Cavell and Philippe Baucq were executed by firing squad. Cavell was 48 and made no protest against her sentence. Apparently the day before her death, speaking to the chaplain who spent her last day with her, she had said: 'I realize that patriotism is not enough, I must have no hatred or bitterness towards anyone.' Thuliez was also sentenced to death but the sentence was commuted to life imprisonment.

Germany's intention in executing Cavell had been to send a warning to others in the Belgian Resistance; posters and proclamations stated clearly that anyone helping Germany's enemies could and should expect the same treatment. However, their action backfired very quickly so that they soon discovered they had handed Britain a powerful propaganda tool. Cavell's execution caused a major outcry, not just in Britain but also among other Allied and neutral countries. Newspapers in Britain, the United States and elsewhere were full of the event, screaming in banner headlines that the barbaric Germans had murdered a pure and honourable woman.

In a letter to *The Times* on 19 October 1915, the Rev Jocelyn Henry Speck wrote emotionally of the 'dastardly execution of an Englishwoman at the hands of an enemy for whom self-respecting nations… can have but one feeling: absolute abhorrence. By this crowning tragedy of cowardice, the enemy has murdered not only a woman in cold blood, they have also murdered chivalry'. He went on to comment that Edith Cavell's death would no doubt awaken the 'chivalry of our young men of military age not yet enlisted', which in a way it did. Postcards and posters featuring dramatic images of the fallen Edith Cavell were widely used for propaganda purposes, helping to fuel anti-German sentiment and the image of Germany as a barbaric nation – already at boiling point following the sinking of the *Lusitania* in May 1915. Her imagery was also used for military propaganda, stimulating patriotic fervour and encouraging enlistment, which doubled for two months after Cavell's death. There were memorial services and concerts, and in November 1915 a new chrysanthemum named after Edith Cavell was exhibited in London.

Much was made of the fact that Edith Cavell was a nurse. Replying to a note from the American ambassador, the Secretary of State for Foreign Affairs Sir Edward Grey, was quoted as saying, 'that news of execution of this noble Englishwoman will be received with horror and disgust, not only in the Allied States, but throughout the civilized world. Miss Cavell was not even charged with espionage, and the fact that she had nursed numbers of wounded German soldiers might have been regarded as a complete reason in itself for treating her with leniency.' (*The Times*, 22 October 1915).

However, as the German authorities were quick to point out, the British attitude towards Cavell's execution smacked of hypocrisy.

While acknowledging that it was hard that a woman had to be executed, Arthur Zimmerman, then German Under-Secretary of State for Foreign Affairs, argued that Cavell had been found guilty of war treason, a crime punishable by death, and that in such cases they treated women and men equally. In addition the German authorities pointed to British treatment of women and children during the Boer War, to say nothing of the way the British government had treated suffragettes before the war. To some extent the German authorities were not wrong; the sentence for espionage or treason was death in Britain, too. Although the British government made much of the fact that they did not execute female spies, in January 1916 an English court sentenced Swedish-born Eva de Bournonville to death for spying, only changing the sentence to imprisonment when the government realized what damaging propaganda this would provide.

Following her death, Edith Cavell became an iconic figure, something that lasted well beyond the First World War. Even today she is often still presented as a pure, virtuous and innocent victim, almost a saint. However, in many ways, this was an image created after her death for specific purposes: in reality, Cavell can be seen as an activist, she had of her own free choice made a decision to involve herself in the Belgian Resistance movement helping Allied soldiers to escape occupied territory. An intelligent woman, she knew what the outcome might be and made no protest herself against the death penalty. However during the patriotic fervour of the First World War it was more appropriate for her to be presented as a murdered victim and one who had died for noble and selfless reasons.

Almost two years later to the day, on 15 October 1917 another woman faced a firing squad, this time in a damp field on the outskirts of Paris. Charged with being a German spy, the woman was Margaretha Zelle MacLeod, better known as Mata Hari. Like Edith Cavell, Mata Hari became and has remained an iconic image but in Mata Hari's case, the image was that of a decadent woman, the 'spy seductress', an image popularized by spy fiction and one that still attaches to female spies today.

Since her death Mata Hari's life story has been subject to so much legend, myth and misinformation – she herself added to the confusion by the stories she told – that it is difficult to arrive at the truth. However Mata Hari was born Margaretha Zelle in 1876 in Leeuwarden, Holland, the daughter of a wealthy Dutch hatter. She initially started training as a nursery school teacher but there was some scandal and she left. When she was 18, possibly wanting to escape from the rigid stuffiness of Dutch society, she took the unusual step of answering a 'lonely hearts' advertisement and in 1895 married Rudolf John MacLeod, a captain in the Dutch Colonial Army, who was twenty-one years older than she was. The couple moved to Java and had two children, a son who died very young, and a daughter. The marriage was not a success: MacLeod was an abusive alcoholic and after returning to the Netherlands in 1902, the couple separated; they finally divorced in 1906 with MacLeod having custody of their daughter.

On her own, and in need of money, Margaretha went to Paris where she completely re-invented herself, initially as Lady MacLeod, but subsequently, in 1905, as Mata Hari, a Javanese princess, with a European father. She embarked on a career as a dancer, performing in the Paris salons. She was a striking woman and her erotic dancing, which she said was modelled on Javanese temple dancing, and her semi-nudity during performances, won her many admirers and soon made her the talk of Paris. She went on to dance in Vienna, Milan, Berlin and Monte Carlo, becoming one of the highest-paid performers of the time. She also acquired a string of lovers, becoming the mistress of many high-ranking military officers, businessmen and politicians in various countries, who provided her with money and apartments in return for sexual favours. Unfortunately for Mata Hari, her lovers included a number of high-ranking German officials, including Griebel, chief of the Berlin police, Alfred Kiepert, a lieutenant in the German army, and Kroemer, the German consul in Amsterdam.

When war began, Mata Hari was in Berlin, initially unable to leave because of travel restrictions. Her bank account was frozen, and debtors seized her possessions. A Dutch businessman gave her the money to return to Holland, which remained neutral during the war. Naively, it is probable she failed to realize what impact the war was having. The heady pre-war days of bohemianism and hedonism were over to be replaced by a puritanical morality, as part of which women such as Mata Hari were seen as a major threat to national security. Mata Hari's dancing, lovers and lavish lifestyle had made her one of the most notorious women of the time and by 1915 she was already being regarded with suspicion by British intelligence.

In December 1915 Mata Hari decided to return to France, apparently to sell a house and raise some money. Travel restrictions meant that the only route was via England or through Switzerland or Spain. On her arrival in Folkestone, she was detained by the British authorities who searched her luggage and interrogated her twice.

Nothing incriminating was found but the British considered that she was 'not above suspicion and her movements should be watched'; she was to be refused admission to Britain in future and her reputation as a courtesan and erotic dancer, plus her liaison with Griebel no doubt contributed to the British authorities' view of her as a dangerous individual and probably a spy.

In 1916 Mata Hari made a second journey to France; although she was unaware of it she was by now under surveillance, notes being made of her telephone calls, correspondence and the men she spent time with, who included French, British, Russian and Belgian military officers. Various suspicions were floating around Allied counter-intelligence including the unfounded theory that she was a trained German agent. Despite this, in August 1916 Georges Ladoux, head of French intelligence, approached Mata Hari, suggesting she might like to be a French secret agent. For a fee of one million francs it was agreed that Mata Hari would obtain an introduction to von Bissing, the German officer commanding occupied Belgium. Mata Hari was to return to Holland and await further instructions.

En route back to The Hague, Mata Hari was again detained and questioned by Scotland Yard when the ship she was travelling in docked at Falmouth. This time she was accused of being a German agent, Clara Benedix. During a number of interviews, Mata Hari denied being Benedix, suggesting various high-profile friends who would bear witness to her innocence and finally admitted that she was indeed a spy but for France, not Germany, and described her meetings with Ladoux. Her story was not believed and when Scotland Yard contacted Ladoux, he denied the arrangement, implying that she was actually working for the Germans and suggesting she be sent to Spain.

Once in Spain, Mata Hari, who continued to believe that she was still working for Ladoux, made contact with the German naval attaché in Madrid, Major Arnold Kalle. Pretending she was working for the Germans, she obtained information about German submarine activity, which she sent to Ladoux; they also gossiped about the progress of the war. She had a subsequent liaison with Kalle, who by now had also become suspicious of Mata Hari and assumed that she was a spy for France. He provided her with some misinformation and paid her a sum of money, which she assumed was for sexual favours.

From here on events moved quickly. Mata Hari returned to Paris in January 1917, had one inconclusive meeting with Ladoux who refused to believe her information, and in February 1917 was arrested and taken to Saint-Lazare prison for women, previously used mainly for prostitutes but now also used to imprison women spies. The conditions were appalling. Over the next four months, Mata Hari was interviewed fourteen times, mainly by Captain Pierre Bouchardon, chief investigating officer, who from the outset accused Mata Hari of being a German agent, probably an agent known as H21 who had been trained in the German spy school at Antwerp. Throughout the many interrogations, Mata Hari, although she often produced contradictory evidence and was vague about dates and events, continued to maintain her innocence as well as pleading for bail and better conditions, protesting that she was a citizen of a neutral country.

During her subsequent court case she returned to this theme, probably somewhat naively saying: 'I am not French so what is to prevent my having friends of any nationality I choose? If I wrote to high-ranking Germans it was only because they wrote to me and I returned their endearments, but nothing more.'

In the climate of the time, with the French army mutinying on the Western Front, low morale among soldiers and spy paranoia raging out of control, the outcome was a foregone conclusion. On 24 July 1917 Mata Hari was brought to trial. The hearing was closed to the public and the evidence called was almost entirely circumstantial and uncorroborated. The prosecution referred to her relationships with military officers, claimed that she had used her sexuality to obtain military secrets, that she was in the pay of the Germans – the payment from Kalle was cited – that she had given valuable secrets to the Germans, and that her actions had caused the deaths of thousands of Allied soldiers. In his final statement, the prosecutor said: 'The evil that this woman has done is unbelievable. This is perhaps the greatest woman spy of the century.' In her defence, Mata Hari continued to state that she was innocent and had always remained neutral. The following day she was found guilty on eight charges of passing information to the German naval attaché, Arnold Kalle, and condemned to death. On 15 October, wearing a pearl-grey dress, stockings, long-buttoned gloves, ankle boots and

'The Third War Council has condemned me to death and it is nothing but a grave error... I have truly not done any espionage in France, it is really terrible that I cannot defend myself.'

(Mata Hari, letter to Dutch legate, Ridder van Stuers, 22 September 1917)

a tricornered felt hat, and refusing a blindfold, Mata Hari was executed by firing squad.

The following day an announcement appeared in *The Times*:

> 'Mata Hari, the dancer, was shot this morning. She was arrested in Paris in February and sentenced to death by Court-martial... for espionage and giving information to the enemy. Her real name was Marguerite [sic] Gertrude Zelle. When war was declared she was moving in political, military and police circles in Berlin, and had her number on the rolls of the German espionage services. She was in the habit of meeting notorious German spy-masters outside French territory and was proved to have communicated important information to them, in return for which she had received several large sums of money since May 1916.' (*The Times*, 16 October 1917)

Mata Hari's trial and execution received an extraordinary amount of publicity even though there really was not much hard proof at all; some months later Ladoux himself was accused of espionage. But given the climate of the time, Mata Hari's execution met a profound need: to expose and punish a decadent woman, and warn others who might be the 'enemy within'. Extraordinary rumours circulated after her death: that she had gone to death naked under her coat, that she had blown kisses at her executioners, even that she had escaped and was still alive. The truth was more prosaic: she was executed and because her body was unclaimed, it was taken to a dissecting room in the University of Paris medical school. Even so rumours continued that she was still alive; even as late as the 1920s the *Daily Mail* claimed that a woman's body washed up on a beach was that of Mata Hari.

Since her death, Mata Hari has been the stuff of legends and fantasies; in 1931 Greta Garbo starred in a popular film, *Mata Hari*, which was largely fictional, and numerous books have been written about her, some of them very scholarly works. The question of her guilt or innocence has been hotly debated. In 1929 the head of German counter-espionage during the First World War denied absolutely that Mata Hari had ever worked for the service and in 1932 the French government admitted that there was 'no tangible... irrefutable evidence' of her guilt. When the dossier on Mata Hari was finally opened, it confirmed that the prosecution's case was very flimsy, which together with other evidence, led one of her leading biographers, Russell Howe, to conclude that she was innocent. But whether guilty or innocent, Mata Hari more than any other woman spy, became an icon and household name; she was and remains the archetypal female spy seductress. As Julie Wheelwright has stated in her book *The Fatal Lover*, Mata Hari 'brought together fears about the enemy alien, the wayward woman and sexual decadence'; in the climate of the time whether Mata Hari was a spy or not, such a notorious and flamboyant woman, who lived on the margins of society, was a threat and once charged with treason, had to die. Her image as spy seductress has remained the stereotype for female spies ever since.

Fraulein Doktor

ONE OF THE MOST intriguing stories in the history of women spies of the First World War is that of the 'Fraulein Doktor', also known as Tiger Eyes, the Queen of Spies, the Blond Lady and various other pseudonyms. There are few absolute facts about the Fraulein Doktor and it is possible that she never existed, although it is generally agreed that she probably was a German secret agent who ran the German spy school in Antwerp during the First World War, training up German agents to infiltrate England and France. She disappeared when the war ended and to this day no one knows her real identity with absolute certainty.

According to the German physician and sexologist, Magnus Hirschfield, who wrote a sexual history of the First World War, which included a chapter on 'Amatory Adventures of Female Spies', the 'legendary' Fraulein Doktor, whom he described as 'a woman with nerves of steel, a cold, logical engine for a mind, well-controlled sexuality, a fascinating body and demoniac eyes', was Annemarie Lesser. She came from Berlin and during the First World War trained German agents, using merciless and unscrupulous methods that drove some of her trainees to suicide, and worked in the field as an agent herself, using her sexuality to seduce and obtain information from various French officers. She adopted various disguises, managed to evade capture on several occasions, until finally escaping into Switzerland, after shooting three men. She was said to be a cocaine addict and apparently had a complete mental breakdown after the war.

Another theory is that the Fraulein Doktor was Elizabeth (or Elsbeth) Schragmuller, a highly educated woman who had obtained a doctorate in philosophy from Frieburg University in 1913. Recruited into the German Secret Service by her lover, Lieutenant Colonel Walter Nicolai, head of German army intelligence, she initially worked in the censorship department and was subsequently moved to the Antwerp bureau. There she ran the spy school, training German agents with an iron discipline that, according to some accounts, bordered on the sadistic. Apparently she insisted that her trainees wore masks during their training so their identities were never known. At one point she was running more than forty agents. When the war ended, she returned to Germany and obscurity. During the 1930s a woman was admitted to a Swiss sanatorium suffering from drug addiction and it has been suggested that this may have been Elizabeth Schragmuller.

Despite doubts about her actual identity, the so-called Fraulein Doktor fascinated spymasters and the media of the time. Vernon Kell of the British Secret Service believed she did exist and thought she must have been a very able woman, and in December 1919 *The Times* newspaper ran an article entitled 'The "Blond Lady"', stating that a colonel in the French counter-espionage service had been able to provide more details about her life. According to his accounts, the 'Frau Doktor' had lived in a hotel in Antwerp, was a 'blond-haired lady', who 'spoke French without a trace of foreign accent' and, according to the colonel's account, 'used to address her "tools" [agents] with a French cigarette between her lips, leaning back seductively in a large armchair.' She lived there with two men, one of whom posed as an foppish Englishman, complete with monocle, and a high-ranking German officer, Keffer. The 'blond-haired lady, besides using part of her time in beguiling poor unfortunates into betraying their countrymen,' also collected information that she forwarded to Germany.

Whoever she was, the image of the Fraulein Doktor was of a beautiful, powerful, sexualized and dangerous woman, a spy in the mould of Mata Hari but more dangerous because she was never caught. Her supposed personality and exploits continued to exert a fascination long after the war. Fictional representations of the Fraulein Doktor featured in various spy novels and she was the subject of a number of films, including *Under Secret Orders* (1937), staring Dita Parlo and Erich von Stroheim. Her character may also have been loosely adapted for two quite different female characters in two of the James Bond films: Helga Brandt in *You Only Live Twice* (1971) and Rosa Klebb in *From Russia with Love* (1963).

Chapter 3

Spying Under Occupation

'The greatest spy organization of the War.'

HENRY LANDAU

Operating as a spy in occupied territory is by definition extremely dangerous, carrying risks of capture, imprisonment, torture and often death. Nevertheless throughout the First World War thousands of courageous women and men in occupied territories ran escape networks for Allied soldiers and spied for the British Secret Service, gathering and transmitting invaluable military information. The British public was unaware of their existence and even to this day they have never received the same attention as those who did so during the Second World War.

La Dame Blanche

One remarkable secret agent network, which operated in occupied Belgium and Northern France was *La Dame Blanche* (The White Lady). A few patriotic Belgians, headed by an engineer named Dieudonné Lambrecht, had formed a small espionage network in the early months of the war. They set up train-watching posts at Liège, Namur and Jemelle and from these provided information about German troop movements to British military intelligence, including information about German preparations for the attack on Verdun. However, in January 1916 Lambrecht was caught and in April was executed. Determined to keep the network going, in June 1916 one of Lambrecht's cousins, Walthère Dewé, the chief engineer with the Liège phone and telegraph network, Chauvin, a professor of physics, and Father Des Oynes founded what was initially called the Service Michelin and later *La Dame Blanche*, after a legendary phantom that was said to foretell the fall of the Hohenzollern dynasty.

A patriotic Belgian banker had provided funding for the network but the men knew they needed to attach themselves to an Allied intelligence service and, after working first with Belgian and French intelligence, in 1917 *La Dame Blanche* attached itself to British intelligence. From then on and until the end of the war, *La Dame Blanche* worked directly with and was funded by the British War Office; their chief or director of operations, based in Rotterdam, being Captain Henry Landau, a South African and member of the British intelligence corps, who in 1935 published an account of the organization entitled *Secrets of the White Lady*.

From its beginnings *La Dame Blanche* was an extraordinarily successful espionage organization; Landau described it as the 'greatest spy organization of the War'. Its organizers had no illusions about the dangers they faced; about fifty spies had already been shot in Liège alone, and hundreds of suspect Belgian or French citizens had been arrested. To ensure maximum security and efficiency, *La Dame Blanche* would need to be well organized and run as efficiently as possible. One of the conditions the organizers demanded before agreeing to be attached to British intelligence was that all members of *La Dame Blanche*, whether male or female, should be enrolled as soldiers. This was unprecedented and fraught with legal and technical difficulties. Nevertheless, Landau agreed to the condition and from then on *La Dame Blanche* was effectively run as a military organization. The organizers divided Belgium into four regions, each with a lead agent heading operations, and three battalions were created with centres at Liège, Namur and Charleroi. Each battalion was divided into companies, of which there were nine, and companies were divided into thirty-eight platoons. The size of each platoon varied; the Hirson Platoon, for instance, had about fifty members. One in every four platoons had the responsibility for collecting intelligence reports from the other three, and for getting them to a designated 'letter box' from where reports went to the organization headquarters in Liège. Special couriers took reports to the Belgian-Dutch frontier, sometimes hidden in specially-made hollow canes and from there agents smuggled them into Holland, which was no easy task as the frontier was guarded by a high-voltage electric fence and numerous sentries. For extra security, couriers and 'letter boxes' rarely knew each other so that if caught, an agent could not betray his or her colleagues. The members of *La Dame Blanche* were referred to as 'soldiers' or 'agents' rather than spies. Moreover, *La Dame Blanche* created its own counter-espionage section specifically to watch the German secret police, whose agents were everywhere and who not only attempted to infiltrate *La Dame Blanche* but also made use of disaffected local citizens as informants or stool pigeons.

Once recruited all members – men and women – took the following oath of allegiance, swearing loyalty to the organization and agreeing not to work with any other espionage organization or to engage in other activities, such as running escape networks for Allied refugees:

'I declare that I have engaged myself as a soldier in the Military Observation Corps of the Allies until the end of the War. I swear before God to respect this engagement; to accomplish conscientiously the duties which are entrusted to me; to obey my superior officers; not to reveal to any one whomsoever, without formal permission, anything concerning the Service, not even if this should entail for me or mine the penalty of death; not to join any other espionage service, nor to undertake any work extraneous to the Service, which might either cause an inquiry or my arrest by the Germans.'

On joining *La Dame Blanche*, members were given a lead disc engraved with their name, date and place of birth and a number. The discs were buried and were to be dug up after the war. Although the British provided funds for expenses, members were not paid.

The soldiers

Recruiting agents for *La Dame Blanche* was not difficult. Despite the dangers involved in spying for Britain under the noses of the Germans, hundreds of Belgian men and women were prepared to risk their lives to do whatever they could to oppose the German occupation and help the Allies. Just over a thousand mainly Belgian but also French civilians of all ages and social classes worked for *La Dame Blanche*, which eventually had agents operating throughout the whole of Belgium and most of occupied France. About 30 per cent of the total were women. Their ages ranged from 16-82 and they included working-class women and aristocrats, teachers, farming women, shopkeepers, midwives and unemployed women. Many nuns also worked for *La Dame Blanche*, including two Frenchwomen, Sister Marie Mélanie and Sister Marie-Caroline, whose convent in Belgium was used as a hospital by the Germans. With the permission of their Mother Superior, the two nuns enrolled in *La Dame Blanche* and passed on invaluable information about German armaments and troops which they obtained from talking with wounded German soldiers.

Women ran the same risks as men. They operated as agents, observed trains and troop movements, compiled coded reports, couriered intelligence reports and acted as 'letter boxes', provided drop-off points for intelligence and passed on information to the next courier. Most worked in the interior in either Belgium or Northern France, while a few operated at the frontier. Getting information – or agents – across the frontier into Holland was particularly dangerous. The leaders of *La Dame Blanche* tended to be men but women ran the same risks and, unusually for intelligence operations, had equal status with men. One of the *La Dame Blanche* battalions was headed by a woman, Laure Tandel, who, with her sister Louise, also a member of *La Dame Blanche*, ran a school in Brussels. Given the ever-present possibility that the many stool pigeons operating in Belgium and France could betray leaders, or that German agents might infiltrate the organization, certain women were briefed to take over as leaders if necessary. Women also recruited agents, set up train-watching posts, and helped to set up platoons.

The women who worked with *La Dame Blanche* did so for many reasons. Giving the lie to Hamil Grant's disparaging views of women spies, patriotism was a powerful motive. With German forces occupying Belgium, it was almost impossible for men who wanted to join the Belgian Army to escape into Holland. As a result, in Landau's words, 'Spying was the only patriotic outlet that remained', and for men being a soldier in *La Dame Blanche* provided their only opportunity of fighting, albeit in a covert organization. Working with *La Dame Blanche*, gathering information or spying for British intelligence also provided women, who would not have been able to enlist, the same opportunity to fight and act as soldiers for their country against the German invaders. Revenge for a son, husband or other male relative killed in the war was another powerful motive, while involvement in *La Dame Blanche*, although dangerous and sometimes frightening, was exciting and gave women a strong sense of purpose. Working with the Resistance was also proof positive that a woman was not collaborating with the enemy, a constant risk for women in occupied territory.

Husbands and wives, and often wider families, worked together within the different platoons of *La Dame Blanche*, which helped to cement the network and also provided a good source of new recruits as one member of family brought relatives into the organization. One woman named Anna Kessler, a widow in her fifties, lost her only son in the fighting in 1914; she joined *La Dame Blanche* and encouraged her four daughters to work with her to help British intelligence. Her service records described her as a 'patriotic and courageous mother'. Different members of the same family sometimes undertook different tasks: while one member of the family took responsibility for collecting information, another might be a courier. Working together as a family was not only efficient but also enabled family members to look after each other. Conversely of course a family unit was vulnerable; if its activities were discovered, the entire family might be arrested, imprisoned or shot.

Watching railways and making notes of German troop movements was the core work of *La Dame Blanche* and provided significant military information for British intelligence about the movement and strength of German forces. By the end of the war there were more than fifty

'A remarkable feature not only of the Hirson Platoon, but of the whole 'White Lady' organisation was family cooperation. Husband, wife, children, even the dog (watching at the door), and often the furniture (a hiding place for compromising documents), each played a part.'

(Henry Landau, *Secrets of the White Lady*)

train-watching posts, each with its own identifying number. As Landau commented in his history of *La Dame Blanche*, 'the work of spying went on night and day', and railways certainly had to be observed twenty-four hours a day, seven days a week. Families often undertook this commitment, working in shifts. From September 1917 until the end of the war Felix Latouche, for instance, together with his wife and their two young daughters, aged 13 and 14, maintained a train-watching post from their cottage in Fourmies in Northern France that overlooked the Hirson-Mézières railway line. During the day the two young girls scrutinized the trains as they went by; at night M. and Mme. Latouche continued the observation. To disguise the information, they jotted down their findings as items of food: beans for soldiers, chicory for horses, coffee for cannons and so on. Completed lists, which were written on scraps of paper, were hidden in the hollowed out handle of a broom that stood against a wall in the kitchen, until a courier arrived. Family groups also provided safe houses for agents, and drop-off points for information, not just receiving intelligence but also passing it on to another group or member of the network. Usually able to move around the country more easily than men, women often operated as couriers. When one male agent, Cresillon, who acted as a 'letter box' and courier, feared he was under surveillance, his wife took over the role of courier. Being a midwife, she travelled frequently visiting pregnant women, and was ignored by the Germans.

Dangers and imprisonment
Covert operations in occupied territory required immense courage and dedication and carried huge risks. The German secret police were constantly on the alert for spies and on various occasions, sometimes successfully, attempted to infiltrate networks. Working as a courier was particularly risky partly because the agent would be carrying material that provided evidence of his or her espionage activities and partly because travel in the occupied territories was very restricted. The German occupying forces had imposed travel restrictions and a strict

curfew, as well as introducing a pass system whereby civilians had to carry identity papers and passes to get from one place to another. Anyone in the streets or countryside after the curfew was likely to be stopped by German military police. Agents at the frontier were at particular risk. A ten-foot high barbed wire fence separated Belgium from France and was patrolled by German sentries and secret police who were constantly on the watch for spies trying to cross from one country to the other. Even so, some daring agents succeeded. On one occasion two young women, Clémie de l'Epine and Marie-Antoinette, both daughters of aristocratic Belgian families and members of *La Dame Blanche* offered to make the crossing to meet with a man who was to found a new platoon. Dressed as peasant women, the two girls, with an experienced guide who was carrying a sack of potatoes that he was supposedly taking to a farm, made their way through thick forest. Arriving at a small farm, they were stopped by Germans who demanded identity cards. Their guide was taken away and the young women waited nervously for some hours. Their guide returned safely but without the potatoes. Continuing their journey, they managed to cross the border scrambling through a hole in the barbed wire barrier. Arriving in France they stayed one night with a sympathetic French farmer, then spent a day travelling on foot and by river to the town of Charleville, making detours to avoid German soldiers. On one occasion, seeing German soldiers in the town, they dived into a nearby house for safety; the occupants were apparently not surprised and gave them shelter. Eventually the two young women made contact with M. Dommelier and Mme. Grafetiaux and passed on instructions from *La Dame Blanche* for setting up a new train-watching post at Charleville. Their mission accomplished, the two girls made their long way home.

La Dame Blanche houses were sometimes raided, necessitating quick thinking on the part of agents. *La Dame Blanche* used a large house on the banks of the River Meuse as its secretariat, the place where reports were typed up and prepared for sending to British intelligence. Acting on information in an anonymous letter, the German secret police raided the house. When they arrived, two couriers were leaving the house; they were seized and the police entered the house where they found Madame Goessels, a highly respectable 35-year-old woman who ran the secretariat, two brothers – Louise and Antony Collard, agents of *La Dame Blanche* – and some intelligence reports. The police arrested everyone and discovered the intelligence reports. During their first interrogation, the quick-witted Mme. Goessels, who did not deny her involvement, claimed that one of the couriers was her lover, who knew nothing about her espionage activities and the other was just his friend. Her courage and quick thinking saved the lives of the couriers, but the

Collards were later executed. Madame Goessels was initially sentenced to death, subsequently commuted to imprisonment with hard labour.

Many other female agents were caught, arrested, interrogated and sentenced to life imprisonment with hard labour either in St Léonard prison in Liège or the German prison at Siegburg. Exact figures are difficult to obtain but probably around 300 women were imprisoned at Siegburg during the war, having been convicted of spying for the Allies. Conditions in the prison were extremely harsh. Until 1917 women were forced to wear prison clothing – ankle-length woollen or grey dresses with aprons and neckerchiefs – and were kept in cells 12ft long, 8ft wide and 9ft high. Food consisted of black bread, a vegetable soup often containing insects, black coffee and thin gruel. Lights were switched off early and women spent up to fifteen hours a day in darkness. Sanitation was primitive – dysentery, typhoid and TB were rife – and there was virtually no medical care. Women supported each other, keeping up morale and nursing each other when sick. They also attempted in whatever ways they could to continue their resistance and defy the Germans; on one notable occasion they went on strike, refusing to make shells and grenades.

Women who were imprisoned in Siegburg included Louise Thuliez, who had been arrested with Edith Cavell for helping Allied soldiers to escape capture. She had initially been sentenced to death but, following the furore after Cavell's execution, her sentence was commuted to life imprisonment and penal servitude. Despite the harsh conditions, she survived the war. Another was Jeanne Delwaide, who was one of the earliest recruits to La Dame Blanche and a significant catch because of her importance in the organization. Arrested in 1917, she was taken first to prison in Namur where she was kept in solitary confinement. Dewé smuggled in a letter urging her to 'Remember you are a soldier. Remember your oath. Deny everything.' Despite seven months of intense interrogation, Delwaide remained true to her oath, so helping to protect the leaders of La Dame Blanche. Brought to trial she was sentenced to life imprisonment and hard labour and eventually sent to Siegburg. Other women too, such as Madame Goessels, refused to disclose any information despite abusive interrogation.

Frenchwoman Louise de Bettignies was among the women who were imprisoned in Siegburg during the war, one of the ringleaders of the aforementioned strike, who was trained by British intelligence and helped Allied soldiers to escape capture. She also collected information from informants in occupied France which she passed on to British intelligence. Arrested in 1915, she was initially sentenced to death but this was commuted to penal servitude and she was sent to Siegburg, where she died in September 1918.

Louise de Bettignies

SOMETIMES DESCRIBED AS the 'Joan of Arc of the North', because of her courage, Louise de Bettignies was born in 1880 in St Amand, France, into a once-wealthy family. She was well educated at Girton College, Oxford, spoke many languages and was a devout Catholic. Accounts describe her as an active, independent-minded woman. When war began both French and British intelligence approached her to work for them but she chose to work for British intelligence, reporting to a Major Kirke. She was given some training in codes and other spy craft, then, under the assumed name Alice Dubois, began to work for the British in February 1915. From spring 1915 a young Frenchwoman, Leonie Vanhoutte – alias Charlotte Lameron – became her close assistant. Bettignies set up an extremely effective network around Lille, consisting of eighty people who gathered a wealth of sensitive military information such as the positioning of artillery batteries, munition stores, troop placements and movements, and information about airfields. Information was passed to British intelligence within 24 hours. De Bettignies headed the team of agents and couriers but also took many personal risks herself often carrying the information, on thin sheets of Japanese paper, to the Netherlands and making frequent trips to Britain. Vanhoutte was captured on 25 September 1915 and imprisoned in Saint-Gilles prison. Postcards from someone called 'Alice' were found in her boarding house. De Bettignies was captured at Tournai on 20 October 1915 as she was trying to cross the Franco-Belgian border using false identification papers. She was initially taken to Saint-Gilles prison, where she and Vanhoutte communicated with each other by tapping Morse code on the walls, and in March 1916 was charged with espionage and sentenced to death, although the German war council was unable to prove that she was Alice Dubois. The sentence was commuted to fifteen years' hard labour and she, together with Vanhoutte, was sent to Siegburg prison, near Cologne, where she continued acts of defiance, refusing to produce arms for the German army and instigating an uprising in the prison. She died on 17 September 1918 from complications during an operation. The British intelligence service recorded that De Bettignies had provided an 'invaluable' service. Following the war De Bettignies' body was repatriated and she was posthumously awarded the Légion d'honneur, the Croix de Guerre, an OBE and the Palm medal – the British military decoration for outstanding bravery. A memorial statue was erected in Lille in 1927.

Sentenced to death

By and large the Germans sentenced women spies to penal servitude rather than death but Edith Cavell was not the only woman who was executed for assisting the Allies. Another was Gabrielle Petit, although at the time her death passed almost unnoticed. Petit was born in Tournai, Belgium, in 1893 into a modest family. Following her mother's death, she was raised in a Catholic boarding school. As a teenager she worked as a shop assistant in Brussels, then when war broke out she joined the Belgian Red Cross to work as a nurse. In 1914 she helped her injured soldier fiancé to escape into the Netherlands, and subsequently passed on information about German troops that she had obtained during the trip to British intelligence. They were impressed, gave her some training and hired her to spy on the German army. Using a number of false identities, she gathered information on troop movements and military technology that she passed on to British intelligence. Gabrielle Petit also worked with the Resistance movement, distributing the clandestine newsletter *La Libre Belgique* and helping the underground mail service *Le Mot du Soldat* which operated between Belgian soldiers on the front line and their families. Petit was betrayed and was captured in February 1916 and charged with espionage. Imprisoned in Brussels, she refused to reveal the identities of other agents, and was shot by firing squad on 1 April 1916. Aged 23, she went stoically and defiantly to her death, refusing a blindfold and shouting *'Vive la Belgique'*. Unlike Cavell, Petit's achievements and execution went virtually unnoticed at the time. After the war, however, she became a Belgian national heroine and a monument honouring her was erected in Brussels and a square in her hometown of Tournai was named after her.

Another Belgian woman executed for espionage was 47-year-old Elise Grandprez. She initially sheltered Allied soldiers and then, with her brothers and sister Marie, acted as a courier and ran a train observation post. She and her sister worked at night writing intelligence reports in invisible ink on wrapping paper or between the printed material on magazine pages before taking them to Liège. In January 1917 the whole family was arrested together with two other agents and Elise, her

> 'I will show them that a Belgian woman knows how to die.'
>
> (Gabrielle Petit. Inscribed on her monument, Place St Jean, Brussels)

brother Constant, and one of their colleagues were sentenced to death and shot by firing squad. It is said that Elise Grandprez, a highly patriotic woman, made three small Belgian flags out of material brought into the prison for her by a nun. As she faced the firing squad, she gave two of the flags to the men with her, and pressed the other to her heart.

Two other women shot on charges of spying for the Allies were two young Flemish peasant women, Emilie Schattermann and Léonie Rameloo, aged 21 and 22 respectively. They lived in a small village on the Belgian-Dutch border and helped refugees to escape as well as acting as frontier guards for Louise de Bettignies and other agents in the Lille area. Caught with another agent, they were executed by firing squad on 12 September 1917.

The bravery and patriotism of women such as Louise de Bettignies, Louise Thuliez and the women of *La Dame Blanche* who risked their lives to assist the Allied cause was extraordinary but despite this most of their names have been lost. In fact, even allowing for some of the post-war memorials, very few people know the names of those involved, or even the existence of the Resistance and espionage networks that operated in the occupied countries during the First World War. The fact that they existed and that so many women risked their lives for patriotic and honourable motives completely challenges and undermines the stereotypical views presented by spy novelists and spymasters such as Hamil Grant. These were not passive women, or sexual vamps; they were by and large 'ordinary women' of great courage and patriotism who were prepared to risk their lives in the extraordinary conditions of wartime and the reality of occupying forces. They had considerable successes: according to Henry Landau during the last eighteen months of the war *La Dame Blanche* was supplying the Allies with more than 75 per cent of the intelligence coming out of occupied Belgium and France. Immediately after the war, their contribution to the Allied war effort was recognized. All members of *La Dame Blanche* were awarded the Order of the British Empire (OBE), usually in formalized military ceremonies in Belgium. Money was also provided to meet expense and hardship claims. Memorials to some of the women were also erected in their localities. Even though there are extensive archives about *La Dame Blanche* in Belgium, the existence of its members is hardly remembered today and the network receives no coverage in most histories of the First World War. The reasons for this neglect are debatable. According to historian Tammy Proctor, their existence may have been played down for propaganda reasons at the time: to have highlighted an efficient and active espionage service in Belgium might have undermined the propaganda image of Belgium as a bleeding, victimized and raped nation; it may also be because the contribution of women to war, as in most fields, is often overlooked. Either way, it is only women such as Mata Hari, portrayed as a sexual vamp, and Edith Cavell, presented as the patriotic martyr, who have stuck in the public mind, rather than the women of *La Dame Blanche*.

Walking a tightrope

One woman who spied for Britain in Belgium during the First World War gained the German Iron Cross as well as French and British decorations for 'distinguished gallantry'. Marthe Cnockaert McKenna was born in Belgium in 1892, and for two years during the First World War she walked a daily tightrope, working as a nurse in a German military hospital while at the same time spying for British military intelligence. After the war she wrote a book entitled *I Was a Spy!* – it was published in 1932 and described her activities as a spy in exciting detail.

Marthe McKenna was born Marthe Cnockaert in Westroosebeke, Belgium, one of five children; her father was a farmer. She studied at the medical school in Ghent but the outbreak of war interrupted her studies and she was in Westroosebeke when it was overrun by German troops in 1914. In her book she describes the retreating French and Allied troops and the devastation inflicted by the invading forces who set a number of houses on fire, including that of her family. Nuns set up an emergency hospital to treat German and Allied soldiers, and Cnockaert, who spoke fluent German and English as well as Flemish and French, volunteered her services as a nurse. Fearful of spies, the Germans evacuated most of the villagers, including Marthe's mother, but allowed Marthe to remain behind nursing wounded German and Allied soldiers.

In January 1915 the German authorities, impressed by Marthe's nursing, sent her to work at a military hospital in Roulers, a small market town near the Menin Road. There Marthe was re-united with her mother and both took lodgings in a house where German soldiers were also billeted. As a nurse, Marthe was given a night pass, which would allow her to walk around the streets at any time of the night should there be an emergency at the hospital; it meant that she, unlike most other civilians, was able to avoid the nightly curfew which operated from 7.00 pm until 5.00 am.

Not long after Marthe arrived in Roulers she found herself a 'participant in strange events of a nature which in my wildest dreams I had never pictured myself taking part'. Early one morning a close family friend, Lucille Delconck, arrived at their house, having crossed the frontier from Holland. Warning Marthe and her mother to keep her visit secret, Delconck not only brought letters from Marthe's brothers but also revealed that she was a spy for British intelligence and wanted to recruit Marthe. Ever since its earliest beginnings spying has always been regarded as an unsavoury profession but despite its reputation, Marthe, with her mother's approval, accepted, seeing it as an opportunity to serve her country and in due course was put in touch with local agents and given her instructions.

> 'I knew what she must mean, a spy, and for a moment I was
> filled with horror. I knew that spies existed in Belgium and
> that they were serving their country, yet somehow I had
> regarded them as things inhuman and far removed from my
> own sphere.'
>
> (Marthe McKenna, *I Was a Spy!*)

For the next two years, Marthe McKenna, or Cnoeckart as she still was during the war, worked at the German hospital in Roulers, nursing German soldiers and the occasional Allied prisoner. She was a conscientious nurse and made good friends among the German hospital staff, who trusted and admired her so much so that having been at the hospital for some while, and ironically after returning from a spying mission, she was presented with the German Iron Cross in acknowledgement of her humanitarian work. Simultaneously, however, she was working for British intelligence, using her position as a nurse to carefully pry out information about troop movements, the positioning of military formations, artillery supply dumps and any military activities taking place or due to take place in the town. She also helped two wounded Allied soldiers to escape from the hospital to freedom.

Marthe worked closely with two other female agents, one of them a 70-year-old woman, known as 'Canteen Ma', who came into Roulers frequently to sell fruit and vegetables and was seen as harmless by the Germans, and who briefed Marthe with instructions from British intelligence, and the other known simply as 'No 63', who was their 'letter box' and smuggled the intelligence passed on by couriers across the border into Holland. Marthe Cnoeckart's code name was 'Laura'; her instructions were to code any information she obtained, and pass it to 'Agent 63', whom she never met. She wrote the coded messages on tiny slips of paper, rolled them up tightly, hid them in her hair or sewed them into her skirt and passed them through Agent 63's window late at night. She relied on her special pass to walk through the town after curfew, but often hid from German military police who patrolled the town. From time to time other agents arrived in Roulers and made contact with Marthe. Described as 'safety-pin men' in Marthe McKenna's account, the agents identified themselves by two safety pins worn diagonally under their collars.

In March 1915 Marthe found herself with another potential source of military intelligence when her parents took over the proprietorship of the Carillon Café in Roulers. Marthe, then still in her early twenties, recognized this as an opportunity; 'Men will talk and boast over strong liquor, and men are also apt to pay attention to the proprietress' daughter. I realized that much useful information might be picked up in this way.' She did however worry that she might draw too much attention to herself. The Germans had already arrested a number of so-called 'café girls' whom they suspected of trying to obtain information from soldiers. Allied intelligence too suspected local women who appeared to be collaborating with the enemy.

By all accounts, Marthe McKenna was an extremely successful spy: she made regular reports about the build-up of troops locally, troop movements, weapon stocks and German military planning, and provided timely warning about a planned Zeppelin raid on London. She took some extraordinary risks, such as searching the room of one of the German soldiers billeted in their house, and the information that she fed back to British intelligence resulted in a number of successful Allied bombing raids. Marthe was often distressed by the destruction and deaths that followed, deaths that included the deaths of German men whom she had known. Following an Allied raid on Roulers train station, she 'crept upstairs... thinking of the smoking ruins of the station and the fate of my little German officer friend of the Railway Transport. The groans of the mangled Germans whom I knew must lie thick about the station seemed ringing in my ears.' Nevertheless, Marthe never doubted that it was her patriotic duty to continue her espionage activities, and according to her account also believed that her nursing perhaps compensated to some extent.

Marthe appears to have won the confidence not only of the hospital staff but also of various German officers that she met and who were obviously attracted to her. In order to obtain as much information as possible she encouraged their interest and dined with various officers and on one occasion even went to Brussels with one high-ranking officer in an attempt to learn whatever she could about the Kaiser who was apparently due to visit Roulers. Not surprisingly, the Germans whom she befriended expected that the encounters would lead to sex but Marthe managed to escape their advances and gain the information she needed. She was, however, realistic and aware that she might not always be able to escape the inevitable sexual encounters, saying in her memoirs, 'I was a Secret Agent, not a ridiculous young girl.'

On one occasion a German officer, Otto von Promft, who was billeted at her house approached Marthe and invited her into his room. Worried that her cover had by now been blown, she was astounded to be asked whether she would act as a spy for the German Secret Service, obtaining information about local inhabitants suspected of being spies. In a 'terrible quandary' and fearing that she might end up being 'a spy for friend *and* foe', and also suspecting that this was a trap designed to discover her true loyalties, Marthe produced some false information and told one of the local agents what had happened. Two days later the officer was found dead, no doubt shot by one of the 'safety-pin' men.

For Marthe it was the 'more outstanding episodes of my life as a spy' that left a lasting impression. According to her own account, these included disguising herself as a wounded German soldier and destroying a German intelligence telephone wire, and a successful act of sabotage in 1916 that eventually led to her arrest. Working with another agent, who had discovered a long disused sewer that ran from the hospital to a German munitions supply dump, she helped to blow it up. A few days later she noticed she had lost her wristwatch. Some time later, the Germans posted a notice about lost property that included a wristwatch. For some reason, and against her better judgement, she went to claim her watch but what she did not know was that the watch had been found at the site of explosion. German military police arrived at her house, discovered two coded messages in her room, hidden under some loose wallpaper behind her washbasin, and she was arrested and imprisoned. For some months she was interrogated but refused to betray her colleagues. Brought to trial, in November 1916 she was charged with espionage and sentenced to death by firing squad. She expected to die but when it was discovered that she had been awarded the Iron Cross her sentence was commuted to life imprisonment. Marthe spent the remainder of the war in appalling conditions in Ghent prison, being released two years later when the Armistice was declared. She returned to Westroosebeke, then almost entirely destroyed, and met a British soldier, John McKenna, whom she married.

Marthe's entire family survived the war. When she was recovering from her prison ordeal, she discovered that she had been mentioned in dispatches on 8 November 1918 by Sir Douglas Haig 'for gallant and distinguished service in the field'. The then Secretary of State, Winston Churchill, awarded her a certificate for her work for British intelligence and the French and Belgian governments decorated her with the Croix de Guerre and the Légion d'honneur. Winston Churchill wrote a highly complimentary foreword to her book *I Was a Spy!* In which he said that Marthe McKenna 'fulfilled in every respect the conditions which make the terrible profession of a spy dignified and honourable'. Marthe McKenna herself said 'Because I am a woman I could not serve my country as a soldier. I took the only course open to me. And let it be remembered by those who disdain the spy, that in every case where I played with another's life, I was also playing with my own!'

Marthe Richer: double agent

THE LIFE OF A DOUBLE agent is particularly difficult: while spying
for her own country, the double agent has to pretend to be spying for
the enemy, something that double agent Marthe Richer defined as
being 'caught between two fires the whole time.' Born Marthe
Betenfeld in France in 1889, Marthe Richer was something of an
adventuress. According to some accounts she worked as a prostitute
before marrying Henri Richer in 1907. Her husband was a keen pilot
and she in turn took up flying, gaining her pilot's licence in June
1913. When war began she and other women formed *L'Union
Patriotique des Avatrices Françaises* (The Patriotic Union of French
Women Aviators) and offered their services to the French
government who refused. In 1916 her husband was killed at the
front and she, a highly skilled linguist, became a spy for France,
operating in Madrid. Her spymaster was Georges Ladoux, who had
also recruited Mata Hari. Apparently the two women met in Madrid.
Following instructions from Ladoux, Richer, whose codename was
l'Alouette (the Lark), established contact with, and became the
mistress of, Baron Hans von Krohn, the German naval attaché in
Madrid. She managed to convince von Krohn that she wanted to spy
for Germany, while surreptitiously extracting information that she
sent back to Ladoux. According to her memoirs Richer eventually
told von Krohn that she had duped him and had been a French
agent all along. Richer fed back important information to the French
about German U-boat refuelling points on the Spanish coast and
the routes taken by German agents across the Pyrenees but when
the war ended, the French government ignored her because of her
affaire with von Krohn. As she herself had said, being a double agent
meant being distrusted by both sides. Richer remarried and in 1933
was finally awarded the Légion d'honneur. She also wrote a
colourful account of her spying career, *I Spied for France*, which was
published in 1935 and became an instant best seller; it was adapted
for a 1937 film starring Erich von Stroheim. During the 1930s she
was regarded as a French heroine but since the 1970s various French
newspapers have questioned the accuracy of her account, suggesting
that much of the information in her book is inaccurate or wildly
exaggerated. During the Second World War she worked for the
Resistance, then after the war entered politics, becoming a municipal
councillor, working successfully to close brothels in France. She
finally died in 1982, aged 92.

Chapter 4

Backroom Women

'She should... be a responsible type who could be trusted to hold her tongue.'

DOROTHY LINE

Acquiring secret information about an enemy's intentions is not only a matter of sending spies or agents into the field; it also involves backroom workers who essentially 'listen in' to the enemy's secrets, intercepting and decoding enemy signals and communications in order to discover the enemy's plans. This work may not be as dangerous as spying in the field but its role in espionage is just as important. During the First World War, whilst some women operated as spies for British military intelligence risking their lives in occupied territory, there was a positive army of hundreds of women who also fought in this secret intelligence war but from behind desks or in the corridors of the offices of British military intelligence, working as clerks, typists, telephonists, censors, decoders and translators, helping to intercept and process top-secret information. Some were completely untrained for the work, others already had clerical experience but all of them made a huge contribution to the early development and operations of British intelligence and the British Secret Service, although until quite recently their contribution was either forgotten or overlooked in favour of those of men.

Twenty years later, during the Second World War, signals intelligence assumed a far greater importance. The nature of warfare had changed. Instead of static trench warfare, military forces on land, at sea and in the air moved at lightning speed necessitating fast, efficient communication across long distances. Radio communication made this possible and every military commander relied on codes and ciphers to send signals that would be indecipherable by the other side. Making sense of these signals was vital. During the Second World War thousands of British women played a crucial role, listening in to enemy radio traffic, de-coding and code-breaking enemy communications at Bletchley Park or in isolated listening stations – Y stations – which were dotted around the British coastline. They carried out their work in total secrecy, unable to tell anyone what they were doing. Their activity did not carry the same sense of glamour as that of spies, but it has been suggested the work they did helped to shorten the Second World War by up to two years.

Early beginnings
When it was first formed in 1909, Vernon Kell's Secret Service Bureau was housed in one room in the War Office and operated with a small annual budget and a staff of not more than ten, including Kell himself. By April 1914 the number of staff had grown to about twenty-four, of whom four were women. Once war broke out, the increasing need to track suspicious activities and individuals in Britain meant a rapid expansion of staff and premises. The Bureau was put under the command of the War Office and given the name MO5(g) and in 1916 became section 5 within the Directorate of Military Intelligence (DMI), so acquiring the name by which it is best known – MI5. The offices were moved to rooms in Waterloo House, Charles Street, Haymarket, in London's West End, and people were recruited for the ever-growing task of tracking and catching enemy spies, intercepting and censoring mail, decoding intelligence and filing data. Traditionally, men were responsible for this spy-catching work, but as war progressed women were also recruited. By 1919 more than 600 women were working for MI5 alone and many hundreds more were employed in the several other sections and sub-sections of British military intelligence, carrying out a range of duties from catering, cleaning and typing through to translating, recording and storing top secret information.

'White blouse' jobs
During the years leading up to the First World War increasing numbers of women had entered clerical work of various kinds. Clerical work itself had been transformed: the increasing use of telegraphy and telephony, new developments such as the typewriter, shorthand, adding machines and Dictaphones, as well as new ways of storing data such as card indexes and ledgers, had transformed the work, paving the way for the multi-tasking information-processing

office. With the growth of large commercial firms from the mid-nineteenth century and the expansion of banking, insurance and communications to say nothing of the new office practices and technology, employment opportunities for women expanded hugely. Until the middle of the nineteenth century clerical work had been seen mainly as a male preserve but as early as the 1860s the feminist and London-based 'Ladies of Langham Place' realized that clerical work was particularly suitable for women and had actively lobbied to promote their employment in that field. The typewriter, which was initially compared to a piano – hence its moveable letters being known as 'keys' – not only helped to transform clerical work but was also seen as a piece of technology that was eminently suitable for women.

The post office was the first and largest government department to employ women. According to evidence within a Report on the Re-organization of the Telegraph System in 1871, the reasons why the post office, and other bureaucratic organizations, were keen to employ women as clerks and telegraphers were that women had quick eyes and ears and a 'delicacy of touch', which made them good operators, that they would take more kindly and patiently to sedentary work than men, and finally that the low wages, which would draw 'male operators from an inferior class of the community, will draw female operators of a superior class.' Coming from a 'superior class', women would by and large write and spell better than men and, in a mixed office, would also raise the tone. Finally – and extremely importantly for employers – while male civil servants would expect to rise up through the ranks and hence earn increasing salaries, women were unlikely to because they would retire as soon as they got married. Also, it was argued that women would be less likely to 'combine for the purpose of extorting higher wages', that is they would not join trade unions, a view that eventually turned out to be inaccurate.

However reprehensible these arguments may seem today, they were widely held at the time and indeed continued to be the reality throughout the First World War and well after. Even so women themselves, particularly educated middle-class women, seized the opportunity of entering what have been described as 'white blouse' jobs. The work was considered to be far preferable to that of a governess and although wages were low and there was little hope of promotion, clerical work offered respectability and financial independence. In 1881 there were about 6,000 women working as clerks in the post office and other offices; by 1901 the figure had risen to nearly 60,000 women in private firms and 25,000 in the post office and other government offices, and by 1911 there were approximately 166,000 women in clerical posts. By 1914, about 58,000 women were working for the post office.

Working for MI5
The few women working for the War Office before the war were typists, who were overseen by male clerks. Before 1914 intelligence-gathering offices were small and had few permanent staff. Just over 100 people were employed by the Directorate of Military Operations, which included intelligence. When war began in August 1914 intelligence operations in Britain expanded rapidly and a new organization, the Directorate of Military Intelligence (DMI) was created in January 1916, which by 1918 employed some 6,000 people. As casualties mounted on the front line and as increasing numbers of men were called up for service – conscription was introduced in 1916 – growing numbers of women were recruited and were soon working in all parts of the DMI, as well as the intelligence sections of the Admiralty, Army headquarters and Foreign Office. The women were mainly under thirty, single, and from privileged – so-called 'good' – family backgrounds. They included university graduates, daughters of naval or military families, and even Girl Guides. None of them had the right to vote – the woman's vote in Britain was not won until 1918 – nor could they hold political office but evidence indicates that all the women who worked behind the scenes for British intelligence during the First World War did so with dedication and discretion.

During the First World War the Directorate of Military Intelligence was divided into various sections and sub-sections. Women worked in all of them. Approximately 600 women worked in MI5 carrying out a multitude of duties from clerical and secretarial work through to filing, maintaining and administering MI5's Registry – a massive card file of suspects and information. Part of MI5's 'H' Branch, from November 1914 the Registry was staffed entirely by women, who kept track of literally thousands of dossiers and cards recording all the spy-tracking activities of MI5.

One woman who worked in the Registry and wrote an account of her experience was Mrs Dorothy Line (née Dimmock). Like so many of the women who worked with MI5 during the war, she came from a 'good' family background and was approached by family friends, rather than responding to any sort of advertisement. Dorothy Line had left school in July 1914, having hoped to try for a scholarship to Somerville College, Oxford. The university offered her a place but not a scholarship and her father, formerly of the Indian Medical Service, was a small country doctor who could not afford to support her at university. The arrival of war however put thoughts of university out of Dorothy's mind, and she determined to play her part in the war effort. She joined a team of other 'girls' working with The Soldiers' and Sailors' Families Association in London, visiting families of men who had been called up to establish hardship needs. She became ill, returned home and then worked as an assistant housemistress in her old school, Bridgenorth High School for Girls, and as a temporary teacher at the Boys' Grammar School. In 1915 however:

'I had a surprise letter from the War Office; the woman head of the clerical department of MI5, Miss Lomax, had put forward my name as a suitable applicant for work in her department. I was needed for an interview. I did not know Miss Lomax and could not think how she knew about me, but a letter from my mother explained matters. Miss Lomax was an old friend of my Aunt Constance Harvey-Kelly and asked her one day if she knew of any girl who would be suitable to work as a clerk in her department. No previous training or secretarial experience was necessary. The important thing was that she should have had some further education and should be a responsible type who could be trusted to hold her tongue. Candidates for these posts were selected by private recommendation and there was never any advertisement.'

Armed with the 'princely sum of £20' for her work at the schools, she set off to London 'with great joy, and blew the lot on a new outfit; coat and skirt, hat and accessories, and presented myself for interview. I got the job.' She was found accommodation in Old Bedford College, Baker Street, which had been converted into a hostel for women doing war work and was sent to the MI5 department at 16 Charles Street, Haymarket, to work as a 'search clerk':

'There was a very large room known as the Registry in which there was an enormous card index which grew daily. It stretched round the room like a snake. To this index came cards with the names of spies, suspects, accomplices and places often with actual addresses, and all kinds of information – these had to be carefully inserted into the right places. Every day there arrived from the different sub-departments files about people suspected of being in league with the enemy. It was our duty to look these up in the card index and try to connect the information in the files. Sometimes through quite a chance reference to a place or person one would hit on an exciting trail and unravel a piece of useful case history. Many other times nothing of value could be found and it gave one a pang to put N.T. (no trace) and initial it and return the document to the original department wondering "Have I missed something?"'

Ironically, perhaps, on one occasion Dorothy found an individual in the card index who was described as 'harbouring the accomplice of a well-known spy'. The individual in question was the very aunt who had recommended her for the job. Dorothy went straight to Miss Lomax and it turned out that Dorothy's aunt, whose widow's pension was very small, had taken in paying guests, one of whom was the alleged spy. The woman promptly changed her lodgings, but not before presenting the aunt with a coral necklace for Dorothy and recommending a hairdresser in London that Dorothy might like to visit. Wearing the necklace, Dorothy boldly went to the hairdresser but nothing happened. Subsequently the alleged spy applied to leave the country but was stopped at the port. Dorothy never knew what happened to the woman but her aunt apparently commented: 'Our counter-espionage department seems to be on the spot after all!'

In 1917 Dorothy Dimmock as she was then left MI5 to get married to Captain James Line, RFC, but not before introducing various friends to MI5 who carried on her work on the card index. Interestingly, when the future Director General of MI5, Stella Rimington, joined MI5 in 1969, she spent time working in the Registry as part of her early training. At that point it was still staffed exclusively by women.

Some 3,500 women worked in MI9, the Postal Censorship Branch, which was responsible for censoring and intercepting mail. Within MI9 women worked as clerks and censors, translated letters from abroad, and tested mail for invisible ink. MI9 handled an extraordinary amount of correspondence, including all non-military incoming and outgoing mail, as well as so-called transit mail, which passed through Britain on its way to other countries. Initially only men, those who were too old or unfit to join the armed forces, were employed to do the work but as the quantity of mail that needed to be examined increased, women were recruited. One of the women who worked in the Censorship Branch was Freya Stark, who later went on to become a very well-known writer and traveller. She joined the Censorship Department in 1916:

'In late autumn two householders guaranteed me and I went on trial as a Censor. This consisted of three weeks' training during which the letters were re-censored by a supervisor. She was an embittered woman who spent her time in a long room full of desks telling us all what fools we were, but at the end of three weeks I was sent on into a building off the Strand, where I worked for thirty-five shillings a week... The letters I passed now went on my own responsibility: if I saw anything suspicious I sent it up with a form where the reasons for suspicion were given, and if the higher department thought the matter worth investigating the form was returned with a red star attached. I used to get from one to five stars a day, but a very stupid girl next to me hardly got three a week so I can't help thinking that a good many undesirable things slipped past her. I could read about 150 letters a day (German, French and Italian mail from or to Switzerland). They were mostly dull; no one would believe how often people say the same thing: we had a cold snap at the time, and 120 out of the 150 letters described bursting pipes. The suspicious letters were, of course, interesting: some one could make sure of – the morse code cut round stamp edges, the lining of envelopes, and the flourishes and underlinings used as guides to key words: but generally it was a sort of *instinct* which told me to look carefully, and I had some difficulty in finding words for my suspicions that I would write on the form: more often than not this vague feeling was right and a red star showed that the clue was being followed.'

Women also worked in Naval intelligence, in what was known as Room 40, so named after Room 40 in the Old Building at the Admiralty. Room 40 intercepted and decoded enemy messages and ciphers, much of the work being focused on German naval codebooks and maps. Information received was top secret. The director was William Reginald Hall, known as 'Blinker' because of a facial twitch, who was assisted by a brilliant codebreaker, Sir Alfred Ewing. Other men on the team included Alfred Dillwyn 'Dilly' Knox, a classics scholar who went on to work on the Enigma machine during the Second World War. During the First World War, Room 40 decoded around 15,000 German communications, its most significant success occurring in 1917 when Room 40 decoded the so-called 'Zimmerman Telegram', a coded message from the German foreign minister Arthur Zimmerman, to his ambassador in Mexico, promising Mexico Texas, New Mexico, and Arizona if Mexico joined the Central Powers. Its 'interception' and publication in the United States brought America into the war.

Given the shortage of manpower, women were employed to do secretarial work, unload the tubes in which messages were received, and help with decoding. Recruitment was strict; only women with naval connections, such as the daughters of admirals or other naval officers, or who were personally recommended by impeccable sources were employed. Elitism played a major part: women had to be of the right social and political background. Many of the women were university graduates – although Oxford University for instance did not actually award degrees until 1920 – and several spoke French and German fluently, a much sought-after skill for the work. Women who worked in Room 40 included Olive Roddam, the daughter of a wealthy landowner, whose fiancé was killed in 1914 and who worked as a secretary to 'Dilly' Knox, whom she later married. Some women stayed with the department after the war, and during the Second World War several returned to cryptography at Bletchley Park.

Women worked in other sections of British Intelligence as well, deciphering enemy wireless messages in MI1B, in passport control, and in MI7, the propaganda section. Women wrote reports, processed, classified and précised the highly secret intelligence that flooded into MI5 at the rate of more than 10,000 documents a month. Women staffed switchboards, frisked incoming foreigners at British ports, and worked as cooks, cleaners and drivers. From 1916 women also ran the printing section of MI5. A number of women, such as Lady Sybil Hambro, held fairly high-level posts, managing female staff and running the secretarial sections. A few women also worked for the British Secret Service abroad in Paris and Holland.

Wages, conditions and discrimination
Hours of work were long and conditions often left a great deal to be desired. Some offices operated twenty-four hours a day receiving and processing information so women were employed on a shift basis of around eight hours per shift. In MI9 women were employed to work from 9.00 am – 5.00 pm with one hour off for lunch and a twenty-minute tea break. In practice though, women often worked longer hours. Similarly in MI5, women were supposed to work an eight or nine-hour day with one day off a week; however they often worked seven days a week, having a half-day off only if pressure of work allowed. Most had one Sunday off in two, but as time went on, female members of staff were allowed one week off every three months.

Offices were cramped and poorly ventilated and, as Freya Stark had

Girl Guides: cheerful and willing

VERY FEW PEOPLE would associate Girls Guides with the murky world of spying and undercover work. But MI5 documents reveal that during the First World War some ninety teenage Girl Guides worked for MI5 as messengers, carrying top-secret material from office to office and even delivering their messages verbally on occasion. At the start of the war, MI5 used Boy Scouts but it was soon found that the teenage boys were far too boisterous, talkative and prone to get into mischief so MI5 switched to using Girl Guides, who were considered to less talkative, although this was debatable, but certainly less boisterous and mischievous. The girls, who were aged between 14 and 16, worked at Waterloo House and two other offices in central London, where they were divided into groups of five or six Guides, each group being managed by a patrol leader, who was responsible for 'the work, discipline and good behaviour of her patrol'. Each day the patrol leaders allotted marks and at the end of the month the group that proved most satisfactory was awarded a picture as a prize. Guides who were chosen for the work needed to be 'of good standing, quick, cheerful and willing'.

They were employed on a three months' probation period and paid ten shillings (50p) a week, with dinner and tea provided. The hours of work were 9.00 am – 6.00 pm and 10.00 am – 7.00 pm on alternate weeks. Guides got one half-day off a week and had to be on duty on alternate Sundays. They were allowed one week's summer holiday and a short break at Christmas and Easter. According to MI5 records, for the first hour of the working day Guides had to dust rooms, fill up inkwells and disinfect telephones. After completing those duties, they collected documents from the post room or took them for posting, ran messages, sorted cards, collected files and gathered waste paper for burning. Some Guides were also taught to clean and repair typewriters.

At a time when women of whatever age were expected to conduct themselves with decorum, Girl Guides had to observe a strict dress code, with skirts being no more than 8 inches off the ground. They had to wear a belt and their hat at all times. Between 1914 and 1918, the Guides carried out their duties with immense devotion. They pledged on their honour never to read the papers they carried, and they stuck to their pledge. At times perhaps their enthusiasm could be a bit overwhelming. In March 1920 *The*

Nameless Magazine carried 'An Essay on the Girl Guide' by M.S. Aslin. Written in a humorous vein, Miss Aslin of MI5 Registry commented that 'the Girl Guide may be found, in all stages of perfection and imperfection, lurking in dark corners of 16, Charles Street. She has many functions. One of these is to snub you when you seek to penetrate beyond the sacred portals of the Office… She speeds from floor to floor, bearing messages… and no obstacle is too great for her to fall over in her devotion to this happy task. Released for the moment, she retires to her attractive little sitting room, where she reads and writes or converses quietly (?) on high topics with her friends'.

implied, women often found themselves working in very close proximity with women they did not get on with particularly well; the work itself, while crucial to British intelligence, could sometimes be very monotonous as women sorted through countless letters and filed numerous documents. Knowing the work was top secret and important to British security did not necessarily lessen the strain and tedium that many women experienced.

Despite their skills and the enormous contribution they made to the running and development of the British secret service, women were consistently paid less than men in all departments, as they were of course in all areas of waged work. For instance female clerical workers in MI5 received between £7 and £10 per month, with one of the supervisors, the same Edith Lomax who interviewed Dorothy Dimmick, being initially paid £20 per month, rising to £29 per month by 1919. Male officers by contrast were paid £33 per month. The same differences applied throughout British intelligence. Female graduates working in cryptography, who were among the highest paid women workers, earned an annual salary of £200, while their male counterparts earned between £350 and £500 per year. Nor were women entitled to bonuses that were paid to male workers in the censorship department. Unequal wages were not the only examples of sex discrimination; women in MI5 had to fight hard to be regarded as colleagues rather than just drudges or skivvies. After the war an S. Callow wrote a humorous poem entitled *Song of the Women Clerks* describing the varied types of work that she and other women had done but implied that despite their hard work and the fact that many women had degrees, they were not necessarily seen as equal to the men. There was recognition at the end of the war but change took a long time to arrive. Seventy years later when Stella Rimington first joined MI5 she commented that 'even in 1969, the ethos had not changed very much from the days when a small group of military officers, all men of course... pitted their wits against the enemy. It soon became clear to me that a strict sex discrimination policy was in place in MI5 and women were treated quite differently from men.'

Top secret

The British secret service looked for various qualities in the women they recruited: women were expected to be well educated and to be of good social standing. Many were recruited from Oxford and Cambridge and women's colleges such as Cheltenham Ladies College. Clerical experience was valuable but not essential and the ability to speak other languages, particularly French and German, was very useful. Women working in naval intelligence had to be the daughters of admirals or other naval officers, and all women recruited had to come with first-class references. Above all, the women who worked in British intelligence needed to be discreet; it was essential that they said nothing about the work they were doing, which was absolutely top secret. As a result women told nobody where they were working or what they were doing. According to Dorothy Line, the roof of the MI5 building, where women sometimes escaped to get a breath of fresh air, overlooked Nelson's column, which from that angle made 'the great Admiral's tri-corn hat look like a pair of horns and his sword like a tail. This was useful because it was impressed on us that it was most important never to say where we worked. So when we were asked by curious relatives and friends "Where is your office?" we could say blithely "Where Nelson looks like Mephistopheles".'

Despite the difficulties, there was official recognition of the work that women had done. Following the war former MI5 women formed The Nameless Club, which kept old members in touch with each other. Miss Lomax was President and they produced a type of old girls' magazine, *The Nameless Magazine*. The March 1920 edition listed the names of fifteen women who had been mentioned in the *London Gazette*, five of them on 1 September 1918 and ten on 18 August 1919, for 'valuable War Services', and a letter from Vernon Kell to Miss Lomax in which he said: 'I was so pleased to see in today's *Gazette* [18 September 1919] that ten of our ladies had been mentioned for valuable War Services in connection with the War. Please give them my congratulations. With a staff like yours, which one and all have done such splendid work, it is always difficult to make a selection.'

Once the war was over, women who had worked in British intelligence, like women in all other areas of war work, were either dismissed or encouraged to go back into the home. Some women did manage to remain with MI5, and many were recruited once more when the Second World War began twenty or so years later. Several women went on to carve impressive careers: Hilda Matheson, for instance, who worked for MI5 during the First World War, and subsequently became Nancy Astor's political secretary, was headhunted by the BBC in 1926. She became the BBC's first Director of Talks, introducing individuals such as H.G. Wells, Bernard Shaw and Vita Sackville-West to the airwaves and in 1929 initiated *The Week In Westminster*, which was initially planned to inform women – who in 1928 finally achieved equal voting rights with men – about the workings of Parliament and featured women MPs as speakers. During the Second World War she ran the Joint Broadcasting Committee.

Station X

Secrecy continued to underpin women's work in intelligence. In 1919 Room 40 was deactivated and its work was merged with the British Army's Intelligence Unit, MI1b, to form a new grouping, the Government Code and Cipher School (GCCS), later the Government Communication Headquarters (GCHQ). Despite its name, GCCS was certainly not a school: it was a highly secret organization whose stated purpose was 'to advise as to the security of codes and ciphers used by all Government departments' but it was also secretly ordered to 'study the methods of cypher communication used by foreign powers'. This meant that its staff worked to break these ciphers. During the 1920s GCCS, under the aegis of the Secret Intelligence Service (SIS), or MI6, was mainly concerned with deciphering Soviet Union diplomatic communications but once the Second World War began, its work was directed at cracking the enemy's secret codes, particularly those of the German Enigma machine.

As war approached, and with it the fear of bombing raids, GCCS moved out of London and set up headquarters at Bletchley Park, a huge Victorian mansion in Buckinghamshire some 50 miles (80km) northwest of London. Bletchley Park was given the cover name Station X, being the tenth of various stations that MI6 acquired for its wartime operations and its head, until 1942, was Alastair Denniston, a code-breaker and head of GCCS. The first code-breakers began to arrive in earnest in August 1939, masquerading as a shooting party. At first there were about 150 people working at Bletchley Park but as the volume of coded enemy traffic increased, more people were needed. It was not possible for all of them to be housed in the main building so a veritable small town of wooden and concrete 'huts', each with its own code number and purpose, were built to accommodate the increasing numbers of personnel. By 1942 some 3,500 people were working at Bletchley Park and by 1945 there were more than 10,000, many of whom were women. Some were civilians, while others came from the armed forces. Most of the labour force was British but they also included American, French and Polish personnel. The British government drafted in some of the most remarkable minds of the time to work on breaking the Enigma code. They included academics, mathematicians, including the brilliant Alan Turing, whose work in creating a code-breaking machine led to the production of the world's first programmable computer, crossword enthusiasts – being able to crack the difficult *Daily Telegraph* crossword within twelve minutes was a highly desirable skill – linguists and chess players. Often described as 'boffins', some of them were extremely eccentric. Interviewed by *The Observer* newspaper in November 2010, code-breaker Rozanne Colchester remembered that being at Bletchley 'was so intense – there were such a lot of very clever and eccentric people shut away in this strange isolation.' As well as code-breakers and cryptanalysts, staff included decoders, translators, machine operators, wireless and teleprint operators, clerks, secretaries and a host of other related staff members. All worked isolated from the rest of the world in conditions of total secrecy.

Bletchley Park – or Station X – was one of the British Government's best-kept wartime secrets. Eventually it was effectively the hub of a nationwide intelligence gathering and decoding network. Telephonists and wireless operators, many of them women and usually WRNS (Women's Royal Naval Service), intercepted encrypted enemy Morse signals at isolated listening stations, known as Y-stations, which were dotted around Britain and abroad. Working night and day, they transcribed the messages and sent them, initially by motorbike messenger but subsequently by teleprinter, directly to Bletchley, where they were decoded and the resulting information, known as Ultra (for ultra secret), was passed on to wartime Prime Minister Winston Churchill and selected Allied commanders.

One of the many WRNS working at the Y-stations was Shirley Cannicott (née Gadsby). She spoke 'fairly fluent French and adequate German' and when conscription for women was introduced in 1941, was initially called up for the ATS (Auxiliary Territorial Service) but was sent to the Admiralty where she was told that because she spoke German she would be wanted in the WRNS. Following training, she was sent to a Y-station in Torquay, where 'we were on watch twenty-four hours a day in shifts of varying length... Headphones on, set on, swivel the dial ever so slowly forward and back, forward and back, overlapping a portion of the dial each time, until the whole sweep was covered... and then the same all over again, hoping – or hoping not? – to hear a noise, a voice, something other than the swish of what is known as "radio silence". We were a generation of young people who had done this same thing nightly on our parents' wireless sets, searching for foreign stations with dance music late into the night... When you *did* hear that voice, it was all systems go... You wrote down everything you could of what you heard, at the same time ringing a bell for assistance... What you took down was sent to the nearest Intelligence Centre.'

Enigma
At Bletchley cryptanalysts and code-breakers worked non-stop to unlock the secrets of Nazi Germany's Enigma machine as well as other Axis codes. Enigma was Nazi Germany's greatest asset and the Germans believed its ciphers were completely unbreakable. Enigma had been marketed for commercial reasons during the 1920s but in 1926 the German navy adopted one version, and the German army later adopted another. By 1935 Enigma machines were standard issue for all the German armed forces and were used to encode military messages before sending them over the radio as Morse code. Incoming messages could also be decoded with Enigma. Enigma was an extraordinarily clever machine. Looking rather like a typewriter, it consisted of a keyboard for typing in plain letters, a scrambling unit of three or more alphabetical rotors that turned the plain letters into code, and an illuminated board that displayed the enciphered letters. There was also a plug board below the keyboard, consisting of six cables. For each plain text letter typed in a coded letter lit up and was noted down. Each rotor had a set of twenty-six input and twenty-six output contacts, one for each letter of the alphabet. These were cross-wired so any input letter would be transformed to a different output letter as it passed through each rotor, so scrambling each letter three times. To make matters more complex, rotors could be arranged in different orders, aligned in any position and set to rotate at different speeds. Cables too could be plugged into many different combinations. Settings

were changed daily according to a monthly codebook. The result was that Enigma was able to encipher messages in literally millions of different ways very rapidly.

The job of cracking Enigma had begun as early as 1929 when Polish cryptanalysts began working on it. In 1932 a Polish engineer, Marian Rejewski, who was working on the project managed to figure out the wiring of the German military Enigma and in 1938 had invented an electro-mechanical Enigma simulator, known as a *Bomba*. Just weeks before the war began, the Polish passed their knowledge onto Britain and France, and from then on the cryptanalysts and code-breakers at Bletchley continued the work. Given the complexity of Enigma, cracking the code was not just a one-off occurrence; with the constant changes in settings, codes needed to be broken again and again, and as the war progressed, the volume of intercepted signals increased dramatically. According to Fred Winterbotham, who was responsible for distributing the intelligence obtained at Bletchley, at the height of the war, more than 2,000 enemy signals were flooding into Bletchley every day, and probably more. Each had to be decoded, translated, collated and forwarded to the appropriate commander in the field as speedily as possible. The pace of work was relentless.

Destination unknown

Women made up more than 80 per cent of the staff at Bletchley. They worked as secretaries, typists, filing clerks, wireless, teleprinter and cipher machine operators, decoders, interpreters and cryptanalysts. They included civilians, some of whom were recruited straight from university, particularly those who had studied languages, or recruited from secretarial colleges as the need for fast efficient typists and teleprinter operators increased. They also included women who had worked in banks, post offices and the civil service. Many women though came from the armed forces, mainly from the WRNS, known popularly as Wrens, but also from the WAAF (Women's Auxiliary Air Force) and the ATS. Wrens staffed the massive *Bombe* machines, which were eventually housed in five outstations: Eastcote, Stanmore, Adstock, Gayhurst and Wavendon. Of these Eastcote, given the security name HMS *Pembroke V*, although it was in a London suburb and nowhere near the sea, housed 110 *bombes*. From 1943 women also worked on Colossus, the earliest digital computer, ten of which were built for use at Bletchley to break the German Lorenz cipher, known as Tunny.

Given the immense security surrounding Bletchley, staff could not be recruited openly. Instead likely candidates were approached or directed towards Bletchley. Only certain people were suitable: recruits needed to be intelligent, adaptable, ideally with language skills, but above all, they needed to be able to keep a secret. No one was allowed to talk about their work, not even to their family. Often new recruits were not told what their work would be, or in some cases, where they were actually going.

Ruth Bourne, for example, who joined the WRNS straight from sixth form in 1944 was put on a train and sent up to the north of Scotland where she did a fortnight of 'square bashing', scrubbing, cleaning, learning to march and being taught naval technology. At the end of her training she, together with a small group of other Wrens, was told she was going to join HMS *Pembroke V* and would be doing S/D X (Special Duties X): 'When I asked "what's X?" people said "Well, it's not Y".' It was to be thirty years before she understood the reference: Y being the Y-stations around the coast where Wrens worked as wireless interceptors, picking up encoded enemy Morse signals, which they took down before sending them off to Bletchley. At the time however Ruth thought 'at least I'll be by the sea with lots of handsome sailors'. However, this was not to be: far from being at sea, HMS *Pembroke V* was just 'an umbrella name to cover the activities at Bletchley', and specifically one of Bletchley's outstations, where to take secrecy a bit further the foreground was referred to as the 'quarter deck', and the Wrens' sleeping quarters were called 'cabins'.

Helen Currie who worked at Bletchley Park on the Tunny code, often asked herself 'How was it… that I was sent to Bletchley Park and worked there for almost three – momentous – years?' She had joined the ATS in 1938 during the Munich Crisis, having just reached the age of 18. Previously she had been working as a typist in London's Fleet Street. As a Territorial she was called up when war started, listing 'typist' as her occupation. In 1942 she volunteered to train as a signals operator:

> '…and was sent to the Signals School in Trowbridge. I was trained as a wireless operator to do intercept work; basically that meant finding a German station on a wireless set by means of its call sign and then writing down (in five-letter blocks) the Morse signals that were being sent by the German operator. It was difficult work. I was promoted to Lance Corporal – richly deserved, I thought!'

Following her training, Helen was sent to London:

> '…to be interviewed by an awe-inspiring gentleman. I remember

only two of the questions that he asked me. Would I like to work in the country? Could I keep a secret? I answered 'yes' to the first and 'I think so' to the second. My young life had not so far tested me greatly in this respect.'

Rather puzzled by this, Helen Currie returned to Trowbridge to await developments. About three weeks later, with one other ATS young woman, Helen travelled to Bletchley railway station where the two of them were met by a 'genial' Sergeant 'Tubby', whose real name she never learned.

Often recruits set off from London or elsewhere with little idea of where they were going. One young woman remembered arriving at Euston with twenty-two other Wrens and asking the engine driver where the train they were boarding was actually going. He told them that 'the Wrens get out at Bletchley'. Another young woman was told she was going to BP (as staff often called Bletchley Park) to attend a course on poison gas. On arrival at Bletchley Park new members of staff were told in no uncertain terms that the work they would be doing was absolutely top secret. Rozanne Colchester's father drove her down to Bletchley and humorously told her that if she ever mentioned to anyone what she was doing, she would be shot. It was a joke but even so every person who worked at Bletchley read and had to sign the Official Secrets Act and were warned that they were to tell no one, not even family members, about their work or where they were stationed. The consequences of doing so, they were told, would be dire.

First impressions of Bletchley varied enormously. Many women remembered 'countless people' wandering around, some dressed very casually in civilian clothes, others in full uniform. There was, however, little time to become acclimatized: new recruits had to start work immediately. There being far too many people to be employed in the main house, most people worked in one or more of the many 'huts' that were built during the war years. There were perhaps as many as fifty huts, with numbers 3, 4, 6 and 8 being the main code-breaking huts. Women at Bletchley remember that each hut was effectively a world in its own right; people did not communicate with personnel in other huts, nor did they visit or spend time in other huts and, of course, no one spoke to anyone about what they were doing. As a result, isolation was a common feeling.

Working on the *bombes*

Many Wrens worked on the *bombes*, huge intricate deciphering machines that reproduced the workings of Enigma. One of the women was Cynthia Waterhouse, who later wrote a piece about her experiences entitled *Bombe Surprise*. She had joined the Wrens in 1943 and, after a 'strenuous fortnight learning naval etiquette, squad drill and scrubbing floors', was sent to Stanmore where she was trained for Special Duties X, a category known as P.5 (*Pembroke V*), then went to Wavendon House near Woburn Sands where Wrens were literally stabled in a converted stable: 'four Wrens to each stable, meant for one horse!'

Cynthia Waterhouse, together with other Wrens, worked on the bombes in a hut in the grounds that was connected directly to Bletchley Park. The machines were kept running twenty-four hours a day, seven days a week; the noise was incredible. Women worked on

> 'The breaking of the German Enigma cipher messages... has been much publicized... The human side of the story of the WRNS involved in the vital work on the monster deciphering machines has not been told in any detail.'
>
> (Cynthia Waterhouse, *Bombe Surprise*)

a four-week shift rotation: 8.00 am – 4.00 pm the first week, 4.00 pm until midnight during the second work, and midnight until 8.00 am the third week, then 'a hectic week of eight hours on/eight hours off, ending with a much needed four days leave.' The *bombes*:

'Unravelled the wheel settings for the Enigma ciphers... They were cabinets about 8 feet tall and 7 feet wide. The front housed rows of coloured circular drums each about 5 inches in diameter and 3 inches deep. Inside each was a mass of wire brushes, every one of which had to be meticulously adjusted with tweezers to ensure that the circuits did not short. The letters of the alphabet were painted round the outside of each drum. The back of the machine almost defies description – a mass of dangling plugs on rows of letters and numbers.

'We were given a menu which was a complicated drawing of numbers and letters from which we plugged up the back of the machine and set the drums on the front. The menus had a variety of cover names – for instance silver drums were used for Shark and Porpoise menus for naval traffic, and Phoenix – an army key associated with tank battles at the time of El Alamein.

'We only knew the subject of the key and never the contents of the messages. It was quite heavy work and [I] now understand why we were all of good height and eyesight as the work had to be done at top speed and 100 per cent accuracy was essential. The *bombes* made a considerable noise as the drums revolved and would suddenly stop and a reading was taken. If the letters matched the menus, the Enigma wheel-setting had been found for that particular key. To make it more difficult the Germans changed the setting every day. The reading was phoned through to the Controller at Bletchley Park where the complete messages were deciphered and translated. The good news would be a call back to say "Job up; strip machine".'

In all cases, accuracy was essential. From late autumn 1942 Helen Currie worked on the Tunny machines, which were housed in 'brick-built huts surrounded by protective walls' in the grounds of Bletchley Park. They were huge machines to which were attached teleprinters: 'the keyboard was the same as that of a modern typewriter and so it was no problem to operate them, providing one had some typing skill', which Helen Currie already had. More ATS women joined the work as war intensified and with it, the volume of encoded material pouring into Bletchley. As Helen remembered:

'We were divided into three shifts to enable the machines to be operated around the clock – one week 9.00 am – 4.00 pm, the next midnight until 9.00 am and the third (which we hated) 4.00 pm until midnight.

'On the Tunny machine there were numbered circuits each operated by its own button, which was pressed to gain the correct setting. The operating procedure consisted of setting up the machine by pressing in the key numbers which were written on the message pad by the cryptographers. All the important code-breaking was done in the next room, separated from ours only by a partition. Provided the machine was set correctly and the coded letters were accurately typed, what came out onto the roll of white paper fitted to the teleprinter was clear German. It seemed like magic at first.

'Even without knowing the language it was easy to recognize German, and just as easy to see that gibberish was coming out when something went wrong. This happened when a letter was missed out, or one was typed that wasn't there. Mostly this occurred when a letter of the coded text had been missed during interception (or maybe many letters if the reception was bad, as it often was). Then it would be necessary to step the impulses on until the text became clear again. This was often a matter of trial and error – pushing the buttons and then typing the text, and only when clear German again appeared could one breathe a sigh of relief and carry on typing. We typed to the end of the German message and placed it in our basket... As time went on, and news from the various fronts was good and bad by turn, the volume of our work (and the number of people employed at Bletchley Park) increased enormously. Our fingers flew over the teleprinter keys. Clever young men hovered behind our chairs reading as we typed, waiting to take the messages away to be analyzed. Sometimes it was taken page by page: we knew those ones were very important.'

Silent geese

Like Cynthia Waterhouse, most women at Bletchley or the listening stations only saw their particular part of the work they were doing; they were effectively links in an information chain and only a few people saw the entire decoded messages and complete intelligence. Nevertheless, virtually everyone at Bletchley knew the importance of what they were doing and when a particular code was cracked and information came through that was vital to the war effort, rumours spread around and there was a sense of achievement. When the war ended and to maintain secrecy everything at Bletchley was dismantled, Ultra files were locked away, and all the machines were dismantled and their blueprints destroyed.

One of the most extraordinary things about Bletchley and its network was that everyone who worked there remained absolutely silent about the work they had been doing not just during the war but also for many years afterwards. Their achievements and their silence were recognized by certain influential people, notably Winston Churchill, who used to refer to the intelligence acquired at Bletchley as his 'golden eggs', and later spoke about the team at Bletchley as 'the geese who laid the golden eggs and never cackled' but the public had no idea that this secret work was taking place. According to many women however staying silent was not difficult: most of them recognized the importance of their work. As Cynthia Waterhouse commented: 'It was amazing that none of this information leaked out, and if it had, our work would have been rendered useless. I cannot remember it being in any way difficult to keep silent. There was only

one thought in everyone's minds, which unified the whole country –
and that was to defeat Nazi Germany.'

For some thirty years the British public remained unaware of the
vital secret intelligence war that had been carried out at Bletchley,
which had played a key role in helping Allied forces under
Montgomery in the North African campaign of 1942, and had
helped to divert Allied shipping away from German U-boats
during the Battle of the Atlantic. With the publication of *The Ultra
Secret* by F.W. Winterbotham in 1974, however, the work of the
women and men at Bletchley Park began to enter the public domain
and the secret was finally out. Remembering the long years of
silence, Helen Currie said:

'There was the state-imposed silence, lasting thirty years. My
family had no idea what I had been doing. I can only describe
those silent years as a fading of memories. If I did recall the
experience, it took on a dream-like quality... Then one day I saw
in *Picture Post*... some photographs of a Bletchley machine and a
description of the work that had gone on there during the war. I
was excited, amazed, delighted. I could now talk about that
unique experience... The years of silence were over.'

Chapter 5

Special Operations Executive

'The sort of person who volunteered was in the main someone prepared to operate on their own with a considerable amount of courage and prepared to take considerable risks.'

VERA ATKINS, SOE

L odged in the National Archives at Kew Gardens, in London, are some fascinating and sometimes poignant documents – the personal files of women who worked as spies or agents for Britain's Special Operations Executive (SOE), the secret army set up to foment resistance, carry out sabotage and acquire information from behind enemy lines during the Second World War. Reading through the files is a very moving experience not least because the contents of the files bring to life the remarkable personalities, courage and dedication of the women who risked torture and death to take part in this highly dangerous covert war, parachuting behind enemy lines, taking on false identities, helping to organize resistance movements, acting as couriers and wireless operators and sending back vital information to London. Some of them never returned.

Set Europe ablaze

The SOE was set up in 1940 following the Fall of France. Between 1939-1940, German forces swept through Poland, Norway, Denmark, the Netherlands, Belgium and into France. Between 26 May and 3 June 1940, more than 330,000 Allied soldiers were evacuated from the Dunkirk beaches and on 9 June German forces launched a major attack on Paris, entering the city five days later. France surrendered on 22 June, leaving Britain and its Commonwealth partners alone and vulnerable. With large swathes of Europe under enemy occupation, in July 1940, following correspondence between the Minister for Economic Warfare, Hugh Dalton, Lord Halifax and Prime Minister Winston Churchill, a new highly secret organization was set up in Britain – the Special Operations Executive (SOE). Its mission was to promote subversive warfare in enemy-occupied territories, or, as Winston Churchill commanded, to 'set Europe ablaze'. SOE would send spies or secret agents out from Britain into occupied territories to gather information, encourage resistance movements, supply arms, provide training, carry out sabotage and harass enemy forces in whatever way possible. Effectively they were to conduct a secret war behind enemy lines. In the words of Hugh Dalton, in a letter to Lord Halifax, dated 2 July 1940:

> 'What is needed is a new organization to co-ordinate, inspire, control and assist the nationals of the oppressed countries who must themselves be the direct participants. We need absolute secrecy, a certain fanatical enthusiasm, willingness to work with people of different nationalities, complete political reliability... the organization should... be entirely independent of the War Office machine.'

Three much smaller units were joined together to create SOE. One was MI(R), or Military Intelligence (Research), which was a secret War Office department whose task had been to look into irregular ways of causing trouble in enemy-occupied countries. One of its officers, Colin Gubbins, a dynamic Highland Scot, with a toothbrush moustache, who had fought in Ireland and written handbooks on guerrilla warfare, was seconded to SOE as head of training and operations in November 1940. Another was Section D, a small sabotage branch of the Secret Intelligence Service (SIS) or MI6, which was concerned mainly with action in countries that were likely to come under Axis control. The third was a propaganda organization, known as Department EH (after Elektra House, its headquarters) but this was later separated out to form another organization.

> 'An organization is being established to co-ordinate all action, by way of subversion and sabotage, against the enemy overseas. This organisation will be known as the Special Operations Executive.'
>
> (SOE Charter, approved 22 July 1940)

MI(R) had been sending agents into Poland, Scandinavia and the Balkans since 1939 with the aim of helping to set up resistance to invading German forces but it had had little success. From 1940 SOE took over the task. Using a cover name, the Inter-Services Research Bureau (ISRB), SOE set up its headquarters at 64 Baker Street, London, not far from 221b Baker Street, the home of the fictional detective Sherlock Holmes, a location which gave rise to SOE personnel being nicknamed the 'Baker Street irregulars', after the gangs of street boys who assisted Sherlock Holmes. The organization, which did have a flavour of *Boys' Own* adventure about it, was shrouded in absolute secrecy; according to one staff officer's account, the cover name meant that people could wander in and out of the building without arousing suspicion because to all intents and purposes the Baker Street premises only housed a research unit. The telephone number too was listed in the War Office telephone directory as 'MOI (SP)', which staff jokingly said stood for 'Mysterious Operations In Secret Places'.

As time went on, and work and staff increased, other buildings were also taken over including Michael House opposite, which was the headquarters of Marks & Spencer and which housed the Security, Photographic and Passport Section, Norgeby House, where staff of the French section occupied many offices and Montague Mansions, as well as various country houses which were used as training centres and to house agents, produce specialist equipment and as radio centres for maintaining links with agents behind enemy lines. A mews building at the back of Michael House contained SOE's code and cipher rooms, which were presided over by SOE's brilliant code master and cryptographer, Leo Marks, who was based in Norgeby House. SOE also had other establishments around Britain, including what was known as Station IX, the Frythe Estate, which was used for weapons research and development, and Station XV, the Thatched Barn, where staff produced suitable clothing for agents going behind enemy lines as well as developing a variety of extraordinary devices and exploding booby traps that agents could use, among them exploding pens and explosives designed to look like animal droppings; they blew up if an unwary person stepped on them. SOE also requisitioned country properties around Britain, which were used as Special Training Schools (STS) and set up centres in Cairo, Palestine, India and Ceylon (Sri Lanka).

SOE came under the aegis of the Minister for Economic Warfare, initially Sir Hugh Dalton and later – from 1942 – Lord Selbourne. Many of their senior staff were recruited from industry or the City. The first chief of service was Sir Frank Nelson. In April 1942 Sir Charles Hambro, head of the Hambro banking firm, replaced him but from September 1943 Major General Colin Gubbins took over as chief of the service, a position he held until the end of the war. SOE was unpopular in

Whitehall and in some parts of the older British secret service. SIS (MI6) in particular was opposed to SOE largely because it saw the new organization as amateurish, dangerous and out to create mayhem and conflict rather than obtaining intelligence in more subtle and traditional ways. They feared that acts of sabotage would draw too much attention to Allied covert intelligence-gathering. Some senior members of the armed forces too were unhappy about SOE: Air Chief Marshall Charles Portal, for example, considered that dropping men in civilian clothes into occupied territory to effectively function as 'assassins' was not ethically correct and out of keeping with what he considered to be the 'time-honoured' operation of placing a spy behind enemy lines. Despite all this SOE went ahead and recruiting began.

FANYs

In 1944, at the peak of its operations, SOE employed some 13,000 people in a wide variety of roles, as secretaries, administrators, trainers, dispatch riders, explosive experts, engineers, wireless operators and – of course – agents. SOE recruited civilians and people from the military; about 3,000 of the total personnel were women. Most of the people attached to SOE had staff roles doing clerical work, helping to train and look after agents, decoding messages, producing forged documents and creating false identities for agents and liaising with agents in the field. Because of the extreme secrecy surrounding SOE, recruitment could not be done openly. Instead, suitable candidates were invited to join the SOE: men were usually found through public schools, universities, industry and, of course, the 'old boys' networks. Women tended to be recruited from the First Aid Nursing Yeomanry (FANY), although they also came from other services.

The FANY – its members never seem to have objected to the acronym – was a civilian voluntary organization, which was first created in 1907 as a first aid link between front-line fighting and field hospitals. Mounted on horseback, FANYs had a medical combat role, rescuing and treating the wounded directly from the front line. They were taught cavalry techniques, as well as signalling and first aid skills. To this day the FANY remain a fiercely independent all-woman organization whose members are always volunteers; until and during the Second World War they tended to be a very exclusive and rather dashing group of women from privileged upper-class backgrounds, often from Army families. During the First World War, sometimes dressed flamboyantly in fur coats and boots, FANYs drove ambulances, ran field hospitals and set up soup kitchens and troop canteens, often under highly dangerous conditions. Their bravery won them several decorations, including seventeen Military Medals, one Légion d'honneur and twenty-seven Croix de Guerre.

When the Second World War broke out there was a move to combine the FANY with other services but the FANY preferred to remain independent. They formed the nucleus of the Motor Drive Companies of the Auxiliary Territorial Service (ATS) but many were recruited for SOE, following an approach to their commandant by Colonel Gubbins who arranged with her to provide personnel for SOE. Most uniformed FANYs worked on signals, coding and decoding and liaising with agents in the field. Gwendoline Lees was one of the FANY signal planners. She, like many other FANYs, was 'responsible for working all the wireless sets and dealing directly with agents in the field, listening for and receiving their "skeds" as they were known, their schedules and sending messages'. FANYs, also provided administrative and technical support for SOE's Special Training Schools (STS) and from time to time looked after and provided some hospitality for male agents preparing to leave for covert action behind enemy lines, a task they carried out with great efficiency. Some male agents remembered, with great fondness, the hospitality and sophistication of FANYs who, resplendent in ball gowns, organized eve-of-departure parties.

Obviously FANYs did far more than just staff parties but whatever their various tasks, their work, and that of those recruited from other fields, was absolutely top secret – so much so that many new members of staff had very little idea what they would be doing until they arrived. Elizabeth Small, for example, had wanted to join the WRNS but was sent to SOE because she spoke French and had excellent secretarial skills. At her interview she was told only that the work she would be doing would be 'interesting'. On her first day she had to sign the Official Secrets Act and was told she would be working in the French section for a Captain Noble; it was not until much later that she discovered Captain Noble was actually Georges Bégué, the first SOE wireless operator to be parachuted into France. The intense secrecy often caused difficulties when friends and families asked about the war work the women were doing. Odette Brown, for instance, was a FANY who worked as a secretary for the French Section at SOE headquarters in London. Interviewed by the Imperial War Museum, she remembered:

'We would say we were in the FANYs and people would say, "What do you do?" We were not supposed to say that our work was secret, which was far more difficult than if we had been allowed to say so. Lots of people worked in all sorts of things in wartime and if you asked them they used to say, "Hush-hush," which meant, "I can't talk about it." But we were not allowed to say that we couldn't talk about it, so one of the cover stories was the FANY Equipment Office. The other was the Inter-Services Research Bureau. That was a bit easier. The FANY Equipment Office made no sense at all. Why did you work all hours? What could you possibly be doing till midnight at the FANY Equipment Office?'

From 1941 SOE began sending agents into Nazi-occupied territories. The organization was divided into different country sections often with its own distinctive initial – F for instance referred to the French section – and as the war progressed SOE had agents working covertly in all the occupied countries: France, Belgium, the Netherlands, Italy, Poland, Yugoslavia, Hungary, Greece, Albania, Czechoslovakia, Norway, Denmark, Poland and Romania. Agents were also sent to Abyssinia (Ethiopia) and South-East Asia.

SOE's French section was by far the largest although there was some rivalry because General de Gaulle, who had arrived in England in 1940 to set up a Free French resistance movement and government in exile, had his own resistance-linked operation, known as RF. F section therefore referred to those agents and operations that SOE initiated and controlled; it was entirely British-run. Colonel Maurice Buckmaster, who had fought in France as part of the British Expeditionary Force (BEF), headed the F section with his deputy Major Nicholas Bodington. Buckmaster's assistant was Vera Atkins, a highly efficient woman in her mid-thirties, who was later commissioned in the WAAF. She served as F section's Intelligence Officer, working closely with Buckmaster and had considerable responsibility for preparing agents for work in the field, particularly the female agents. She cared for the women agents, looked after their personal affairs and, following the war, set off on a long and arduous task to discover what had happened to agents who had not returned. Within SOE she was seen as a very powerful personality, who achieved almost legendary fame. There were also three smaller French sections: EU/P section which worked with the Poles in France, DF section which set up escape routes and, from 1942, AMF, which was based in Algiers and operated in Southern France.

Suitable work for women
During the course of the war, SOE sent about 5,000 agents into Nazi-occupied territory. Initially only men were sent out but from 1942 it was decided to use women as well, particularly in France. There was some opposition but Colonel Gubbins was very keen: he believed that women could do the work just as well as men and had the greater advantage

Vera Atkins

BORN VERA MARIA Rosenburg in Romania in 1907, Vera Atkins was one of SOE's most significant and remarkable personalities. She came from a wealthy family of Jewish Ukranian origin and studied modern languages at the Sorbonne. She was widely travelled and by 1934 was working in Bucharest as a personal assistant to the head of a large oil company. During this period she made a number of contacts with people in British intelligence, to which she provided information. Owing to the growth of anti-Semitism, in 1937 Vera and her mother left Romania for England and settled in Winchelsea, Sussex; changing their surname to Atkins. Vera joined SOE in April 1941, having been invited to do so by Leslie Humphreys, whom she had known in Bucharest and who was now the first head of SOE's French section. She became an intelligence officer in F section and assistant to Maurice Buckmaster, section head from September 1941. She was indispensable to Buckmaster, who described her as 'extremely intelligent, able and reliable.' She helped to interview potential agents, organized and was involved in their training and helped to plan their reception in France. Vera Atkins also provided cover stories for agents and added essential details such as photos, letters and mementos to keep in their wallets, so creating verisimilitude to their undercover identities. No effort was too great: she poured over every tiny detail of French life during the occupation to keep herself up to date with rations, curfew hours, food stuffs, clothing and so on, on one occasion telling an agent to go to the dentist to have his teeth done in the French manner. Vera Atkins was dedicated and loyal to her agents, who were, after all, facing the most enormous risks and quite likely going to their deaths. She saw them off, took care of their personal details, organized their pay and wills, made sure personal possessions were kept safely, wrote to their families, and organized coded messages via the French section of the BBC so that agents in the field had information about family members left behind. She was quite a controversial person; some saw her as rather unemotional and distant but most of her female agents saw her as their friend and confidante. Families too turned to her for help; the mother of one of the agents who was shot in Dachau, Yolande Beekman, addressed Vera Atkins as 'dear Miss Atkins' in a letter asking for information.

86

Vera Atkins' sense of responsibility for her agents continued after the war, when she set off into ruined Europe to trace the fates of the 118 agents of F section who did not return. In an interview she once said that she felt she owed them that effort. She discovered the fates of 117 out of the 118 who were missing and was perhaps particularly concerned to discover the fates of thirteen missing women – she referred to them as 'our girls' – interviewing and taking written statements from men who had worked at concentration camps, prisoners who had shared cells with some of the women, SOE agents such as Brian Stonehouse, who was confined at Nazweiler concentration camp and had managed to witness the arrival of four SOE agents – Andrée Borrel, Vera Leigh, Diana Rowden and Sonya Olschanezky – who were executed there. In order to do this work Vera Atkins was given the rank of squadron officer in the WAAF, having finally gained British citizenship in 1944. Following her long journey through war-torn Germany, she produced detailed reports of her findings, which she sent to the War Crimes Office of the British Army, and these together with letters of condolence were passed to the families of agents who had lost their lives. The confessions she obtained from Rudolf Hoess – former commandant of Auschwitz – were used in evidence during the Nuremberg Trials.

From 1947 until 1961 Vera Atkins worked for UNESCO, then took early retirement. She was closely involved with the Special Forces Club in Knightsbridge, London, which was set up in 1946 by surviving SOE members, becoming its vice-president in 1996. In 1995 Vera Atkins received official recognition of her work when she was awarded the Légion d'honneur; two years later she was awarded a CBE. She died in Hastings on 24 June 2000.

that in occupied France women apparently going about their daily chores would be less noticeable than men. SOE operations in the field were organized around a system of networks, known as circuits, each of which covered a particular area in France. Circuits were given various code names such as *Jockey*, a circuit in south-east France, or *Prosper*, which operated around Paris and in north-west France. Many of the circuits had the same code name as their organizer. Some of the circuits, such as *Prosper*, which became the largest, also had sub-circuits.

At the hub of each circuit were three key positions: an organizer, a courier and a wireless operator, each of whom was usually recruited and trained in Britain. The job of the organizer, in most cases a male agent, was to make contact with local people who were either already in the Resistance or who were keen to get a group organized, and to supply local Resistance groups with training, weapons and other supplies. The organizer also pinpointed sabotage targets such as railway lines, factories, weapons dumps and dams. Wireless operators were responsible for maintaining links with London, tapping out coded messages providing up to date information from the field, and arranging for supplies and weapons to be dropped in France. They also received coded messages from London with information about new agents and supplies that were to be dropped in their area. It was a particularly dangerous task: the wireless transmitters themselves were bulky, often with very long aerials, and had to be carried everywhere. The operator needed to be absolutely familiar with his or her coding system and had to code, send and receive messages as quickly as possible at very specific and scheduled times (these were known as 'skeds'), while all the time German signal-detecting devices were constantly patrolling the area. The risk of being detected was very high: at a rough estimate, wireless operators were not expected to survive for more than six weeks before being discovered. Couriers were responsible for carrying messages, weapons, money and other items between circuits, often over long distances, travelling either on foot, by bicycle or by train; there were no other means of communication in the field. Couriers were constantly on the move, and therefore subject to the risks of police or army checks and travel restrictions. In Gubbins' view women were eminently suitable for this role: given appropriate cover stories, they would be less likely to arouse suspicion. As time went on women were also used as wireless operators.

> 'Being a woman has great advantages if you know how to play the thing right... I believe that all the girls, the women who went out, had the same feeling. They were not as suspect as men, they had very subtle minds when it came to talking their ways out of situations, they had many more cover stories... Also, they're very conscientious... They were wonderful wireless operators and very cool and courageous.'
>
> (Vera Atkins, SOE)

There was however still a legal problem. Women in the Allied armed services were banned from taking part in armed combat and, by definition, SOE agents were conducting a guerrilla war. Here again Gubbins found a solution, which was to call on the FANY; being a civilian organization its members were effectively outside the rules that applied to the other services: there was no restriction on the use of weapons. As a result, women who were recruited as agents were commissioned as FANY officers for their time behind enemy lines. It was also hoped if women agents held a rank in the FANY it might offer protection under the Geneva Convention but this soon turned out not to be the case: if captured, women, like men, faced the possibility of death whether they were in the FANY or not. Some female agents, among them Noor Inayat Khan, Yolande Beekman, Lilian Rolfe, Yvonne Cormeau and Diana Rowden, were recruited from the WAAF but once brought into SOE were given FANY commissions. Three of the women agents commissioned into the FANY – Odette Sansom, Violette Szabo and Noor Inayat Khan – were awarded the George Cross after the war, the last two posthumously.

Captain Selwyn Jepson was SOE's senior recruiting officer. In an interview for the Imperial War Museum's sound archives, he said that he was responsible for recruiting female agents, despite considerable opposition from 'the powers-that-be, who said that, under the Geneva Convention were not allowed to take combatant duties which they regarded resistance work in France as being.' However in his view, 'women were much better than men for the work. Women… have a far greater capacity for cool and lonely courage.' He took the matter to Winston Churchill, who growled a yes and wished him good luck. To some extent the decision was nodded through but Jepson took it as certain, and recruitment for women began.

Being recruited

SOE recruited some remarkable women, most of whom were sent into France. They came from very diverse backgrounds, classes and nationalities. They included journalists, shop workers, clerks, saleswomen and an Indian princess. Many such as Diana Rowden and Vera Leigh, who were both sent into France in 1943, were British; others had British-French nationality. SOE also recruited a number of Frenchwomen, many of whom had already worked with the French Resistance. They included Andrée Borrel and Madeleine Damerment, both of whom had worked with the French resistance, risking their lives helping Allied airmen to escape from occupied France. Andrée Borrel was credited with helping about 600 shot-down airmen before arriving in England; Madeleine Damerment had been betrayed and had escaped to England before volunteering for SOE. Other women included Virginia Hall – an extremely daring American woman with a wooden leg that she nicknamed 'Cuthbert'; this did not slow her down; the Germans considered her to be one of the most dangerous of the Allied spies – New Zealand born Nancy Wake, who went on to become one of the most highly-decorated Allied servicewomen, Polish-born Krystyna Skarbek (aka Christine Granville), Mauritian Lisé de Baissac and a Hungarian Jew and poet, Hannah Szenes, who joined SOE in 1943 and was parachuted into Yugoslavia to assist a partisan group. She was captured, tortured and executed in 1944.

SOE's women agents included single and married women, privileged and not-so privileged women. Violette Szabo, for example, whose life as an agent was the subject of the film *Carve her Name with Pride* (1958) and who was awarded a posthumous George Cross, was the daughter of a French mother and English car dealer. She had worked as a shop assistant on the perfume counter of what is now Morley's department store in Brixton before the war. She was also a mother with a young child named Tania. Other agents had children too, including Odette Sansom and Yvonne Cormeau. Women's motives for volunteering for this extraordinarily dangerous work varied: most were very idealistic; they hated Nazism and felt that it was their absolute duty to do their bit for the Allied war effort. Some, such as Yvonne Cormeau and Violette Szabo, also volunteered out of loyalty or revenge for the loss of a husband or fiancé killed in the war. Most of the women who volunteered for SOE were young: Violette Szabo was 23 when she was parachuted into France; Christine Granville was 24 and Noor Inayat Khan was 29, but there were also some older women such as Yvonne Ruddelat, who, aged 45, was one of SOE's oldest agents.

Finding suitable agents was not a simple matter and it had to be done in complete secrecy; most usually it was the SOE who approached suitable candidates rather than being approached. Because SOE sent most of its women agents to France the ability to speak French fluently was an absolute priority. Senior SOE staff cast their net fairly wide, keeping a careful eye on women in the armed forces, particularly the WAAF, making notes of women who had spent long periods of time in France, knew the country well, spoke the language fluently and could pass themselves off as French.

Noor Inayat Khan, for instance, was found this way: her father was Indian and her mother was an American. The family had spent many years in France and she was a fluent French speaker. She joined the WAAF in November 1940 where she gained a reputation for being a first-class wireless and Morse code operator. Seeing her as a potential recruit, SOE approached Noor Inayat Khan in November 1942.

The SOE also found Yvonne Cormeau through the WAAF. Born in China, educated in Brussels and Edinburgh, she spoke both English and French fluently and also spoke Spanish and German. In 1940 her

90

Odette Sansom

ODETTE SANSOM BECAME one of SOE's best-known female agents; she was one of the very few to survive capture and imprisonment and is the only woman to date to have received the George Cross while still alive. She was born Odette Brailly in Amiens, France, in 1912. Her father, a bank manager, was killed at Verdun during the First World War and her family was intensely patriotic, a quality that she inherited. When she was 19 she married an Englishman, Roy Sansom. They moved to England and had three children. When war broke out Roy joined the Army and in 1940 Odette and her children moved to Somerset where her mother-in-law lived. The news from France was bad and she wanted to do more to help the war effort. She responded to a radio appeal for photographs of France and on being summonsed to London was surprised to find herself being interviewed by what turned out to be the SOE. Given her fluency in French, her knowledge of France, and her patriotism she was invited to volunteer to return to France as an agent working behind enemy lines. It was a difficult decision but in the event she felt it was her patriotic duty, so despite leaving her daughters behind, which she said was 'heartbreaking', she embarked on SOE's training course in May 1942. In October 1942, after various false starts, she was sent to the South of France, travelling from Gibraltar by boat with two other women agents, Mary Herbert and Marie-Therese le Chene.

Operating under the code name 'Lise', her cover story was that she was a widowed Frenchwoman, Madame Odette Metayer. She was attached to the *Spindle* network in Cannes, led by a dynamic agent Peter Churchill (code name Raoul). At this time the *Spindle* network was in serious disarray; Churchill and his wireless operator had quarrelled, there had been a number of arrests, and in November German occupation of the Vichy zone had extended to include the Riviera, making Cannes a very dangerous place. Odette worked as a courier for Peter Churchill, as well as organizing and attending supply drops. The arrests continued, and in 1943 Churchill, Odette and others in the network were betrayed by a French double agent and captured. She was brutally interrogated fourteen times, her toenails were pulled out and her back was burned, but she refused to disclose any information about Churchill and the other agents. She told her interrogators she was the circuit leader and that she was married to Peter Churchill, who was the nephew of British Prime Minister

Winston Churchll, which he was not. She was condemned to death but never deviated from her story nor gave any information about the network: the sentence was not carried out, probably because of fear of reprisals. She endured two years' imprisonment, in Fresnes prison near Paris, in Karlsruhe prison, Germany, and, ultimately, in Ravensbrück concentration camp where she was placed in solitary confinement, which she survived 'from one minute to the next'. Conditions in Ravensbrück were appalling and she suffered dysentery, scurvy and tuberculosis, managing somehow through sheer force of will to stay alive. According to her accounts, she also thought of her daughters. Amazingly she escaped the mass extermination of prisoners in April 1945 just before the camp was liberated, when the camp commandment, who had believed her story about Churchill, drove her to the nearest American troops, hoping to use her as a hostage. She was very ill for some while after the war but fought back to health and died in 1995. In 1946 she was awarded the George Cross: the announcement in the *London Gazette* of Friday, 16 August 1946 stated that 'The Gestapo tortured her most brutally... Mrs Sansom, however, continually refused to speak and by her bravery and determination, she not only saved the lives of two officers but also enabled them to carry on their most valuable work. During the period of over two years in which she was in enemy hands, she displayed courage, endurance and self-sacrifice of the highest possible order.' In 1951 a film, *Odette*, was released starring Anna Neagle.

husband, who was in the RAF, was killed in a London air raid, ironically while at home recovering from being wounded, leaving her on her own with a school-age child. She joined the WAAF and was posted to an RAF bomber station in Lincolnshire and, given her ability with languages, was approached by SOE. In an interview for the Imperial War Museum Yvonne Cormeau said:

'After my husband was killed I joined the WAAF... going into the forces, one had to fill in a great number of questionnaires and when they asked, "What have you as special qualities?" I put down my knowledge of German and Spanish and bilingual French. After a while this got through the Ministry, of course, and then, as they were looking for people for SOE, I was interrogated. I got a telex from London asking that I should come down to town to see a certain Captain Selwyn Jepson.'

Sometimes chance played a part: Odette Sansom, a French-born woman married to an Englishman and who had lived in England since 1932, came to SOE's attention when she heard an appeal on the radio for anyone who had photographs of a particular part of the French coast to send them to an address in London. She duly sent in some photographs, she later believed possibly to the wrong address, and some weeks after got a letter thanking her and asking her to come to London for an interview. Assuming this was to collect her photographs, she was rather surprised to be asked a lot of questions. She subsequently received a letter inviting her to a second interview: the SOE had made enquiries about her and believed she had excellent agent potential.

Interviews

Once SOE had spotted potential recruits, they were sent a note or telex inviting them for an interview in London, although they were not told why. Interviews were usually conducted in a bleak room often in the Victoria Hotel in Northumberland Avenue. There was virtually no furniture, just two folding chairs, a naked light bulb and a blackout screen. Selwyn Jepson, who in his civilian life wrote thrillers, was the recruiting officer for F section and carried out literally hundreds of interviews, dressed either in civilian clothes or in uniform – he was a major in the Buffs. He usually started the first interview in English then, being bilingual himself, switched to French; any recruit who at this point had difficulty in speaking French was usually politely asked to leave.

Jepson was an extremely skilled interviewer and excellent judge of character; he was particularly skilled at spotting just the right agent. He said himself that he could assess the suitability of a candidate within thirty seconds and rarely made a mistake. The first interview was usually fairly low-key; Jepson would already know a great deal about the woman in front of him and his aim was to establish character and motive: he needed to know that the woman in front of him was not reckless, running away from personal problems or acting from an obsessive need for revenge. A good agent needed to be loyal, cool and capable of taking initiative, but not impulsive or reckless. Courage, prudence and the ability to plan in advance and take initiative were desirable character traits; recklessness and impulsiveness were not. It was vital to find the right person: agents in the field would be under constant strain and danger; it was essential to ensure that agents would not put themselves or their circuit at unnecessary risk.

If the first interview was satisfactory, a second interview was arranged. In the meantime SOE ran security checks through MI5 to ensure the candidate's loyalty and discover whether there were any security risks. During the second interview, Jepson opened up much more about the type of work involved, looking to establish whether the candidate was interested in working closer to the enemy, that is in France, and whether she would be prepared to undertake subversive activities, which would put her life at risk, although still without exactly spelling out what the task would be. Some women guessed: Odette Sansom for instance realized what the nature of the work would be during her second interview and volunteered immediately. At this point Jepson also probed into family commitments. Several women had children but nevertheless were keen to volunteer, and Jepson needed to know what arrangements would be made. Children were not the only concern: Noor Inayat Khan, for instance, was very close to her mother, and was extremely anxious about how she would handle the separation.

Jepson also emphasized the drawbacks and dangers of the work and the strong possibility of not returning. At that time it was estimated that the chances of an agent surviving were considered to be about 50/50. At the end of the war, it was discovered that of the 470 agents that F section sent into the field, 118 failed to return, 117 of them having been killed, so the odds of being killed were one in four. Jepson also stressed the difficulties of a covert role in Nazi-occupied territory; not only was the country swarming with Gestapo and police but also agents would have no contact with their family and friends, they could never tell anyone what they were doing, there were no holidays and no financial reward, just normal service pay. Jepson suggested that the candidate should go away and think about what was involved before making a final decision. He stressed that no matter what the decision, the interview had to remain absolutely secret; the candidate could not mention it to anyone – neither family nor friends. The prospective agent had to make up her mind completely alone and independently.

Finally there was a third interview at which candidates made their final decision, although, as in the case of Odette Sansom, a third interview was not always necessary. At this stage most candidates volunteered; very few refused. They had to sign the Official Secrets Act and were told they would need to join the FANY.

Training
Once recruited, potential agents were sent on what was a very intensive training course at one of SOE's Special Training Schools (STS). Women and men trained together. According to M.R.D. Foot, the official historian of the SOE in France, training could be compared to a 'set of sieves, each one with a closer mesh than the one before', and was designed to weed out unsuitable candidates.

Training began with a two to three week course in one of the country houses requisitioned by SOE for this purpose. One of the best known was Wanborough Manor, near Guildford. Initial training included plenty of physical fitness work with cross-country runs and other exercises, basic map-reading skills and some weapons training, using pistols and sub-machine guns. Recruits who got through the initial training went on to a far more gruelling three or four weeks paramilitary training at Arisaig, a remote area on the west coast of Scotland, where they learned how to strip, reassemble, load, fire and maintain a variety of weapons. These included Colts and Sten guns and agents were taught to fire using a so-called double tap system, pointing the gun, tucking the firing arm into the hip, always firing two shots They also learned unarmed combat and silent killing – creeping up silently behind someone and killing the person with a knife. Agents were taught sabotage techniques, practising demolition and the use of explosives, blowing up locomotives and rolling stock, provided by the London, Midland and Scottish Railway. They learned how to set an ambush and how to storm a house. Sabotage was one of SOE's main aims: it played an important role in France ahead of the Normandy landings in 1944.

Those who completed paramilitary training went on to the third stage, staying in a number of country houses around Beaulieu Manor in the New Forest, often known to SOE as the 'finishing school'. Here agents were prepared for the actual business of how to survive in Nazi-occupied territory: they were given detailed information not just about German army and Gestapo uniforms and ranks but also about the different policing systems: in Vichy France, for example, there were fifteen separate police forces – agents being sent to France needed to know every detail of titles and uniforms. They were given advice on how to cope with sudden police checks: agents who had returned from France provided first-hand accounts of what it felt like to have identity papers gone through. A key piece of advice was never to volunteer any more information than asked for. Lodged in The National Archives is a training manual from Beaulieu (KV 4/172) that spells out in detail what agents had to learn for survival in the field. They had to avoid being conspicuous at all costs: this meant studying local customs and regulations in minute detail – not just knowing about curfews, identity papers, ration cards and travel restrictions but also smaller everyday details such as leaving their knives and forks beside a plate after eating, not putting them by the side of the plate, which was an English habit; drinking soup from the tip of the spoon, rather than from the side; not tucking a handkerchief into a sleeve – again a very English habit; and removing tobacco stains from their fingers because the French did not smoke Virginia tobacco. In fact agents were advised to give up smoking because tobacco was scarce in France but there is no record of how many did. Interviewed after the war, Yvonne Cormeau remembered:

'They gave us some ideas about living and operating in France but they said, "You've got to judge. When you're on the spot things might change. All we can tell you is there may be certain days of the week when you can't have certain drinks or foods in certain cafes, so don't ask. Just try and look out and see what is on the menu and advertised for those days. Please don't do too much dying of your hair or have very noticeable make-up or things like that because you'll fall foul at some time or other. Try and dress as they do locally as much as possible. If you're going to live in the country, don't have manicure".'

Attention to detail was essential. Interestingly, when Yvonne Cormeau left for France in 1943, she left her engagement and wedding ring behind in England. About three months after arriving in France, a 'very observant woman' asked her if she were married because there was a shiny line on her finger, where the ring had been.

Instructors at Beaulieu taught agents how to live their cover, described in the training manual as 'the life lived and the activities patently indulged in by an Agent to conceal his subversive activities'. Each agent was given a cover story; some of these wove in true facts. Noor Inayat Khan's back-story for instance included the fact that she had studied child psychology at the Sorbonne, which she had. Agents were told never to improvise or change their cover, to practise their false signatures and in effect to become their cover, living and working within their false identities, not an easy task. They also learned 'tradecraft', classic espionage techniques such as how to use passwords when making contact with other agents or sympathizers, how to drop messages off at given points without attracting attention, how to carry out surveillance, how to spot and lose someone who was trailing them, and how to set up and arrange safety checks. They were given advice on how to set up networks in the field and recruit local agents, what to look for, and how to approach them, and how to recruit and work with local Resistance fighters.

Interrogation too was also covered: the training manual described various types of interrogation with particular emphasis on interrogation by the Gestapo and giving advice on the types of questions that would be used and how to have an alternative cover story for an emergency. They covered some of the more brutal interrogation techniques and, to add reality, from time to time in the middle of the night, trainee agents would be woken up brutally, dragged from their rooms and put in front of men in Gestapo uniforms, made to stand or hold a chair above their heads and interrogated for hours on end, their cover stories challenged and tested. After some hours trainees were released and it became clear that the 'interrogators' were acting a part. Some of the agents found the process quite amusing but others found it only too realistic. Noor Inayat Khan, for instance, found her role-play interrogation very frightening. All agents were told that if captured, they were expected to hold out under torture for forty-eight hours so that members of their circuit still at large could get to places of safety, change passwords, and destroy any incriminating evidence.

During the final stage of training, agents were sent to Ringway airport near Manchester, where they learned how to parachute out of a plane, which in itself could be very nerve-wracking. Finally, agents were given a mock 'mission' to carry out, which could run over several days. Students were sent off with a given task, perhaps to steal weapons or place explosives; built into the 'mission' might be police or other checks, the need to contact people and pass on information, and to find accommodation. The aim was to give a flavour of being in occupied territory. Noor Inayat Khan was given a ninety-six-hour mission which involved going to Bristol, making contact with and recruiting 'agents', setting up a safe 'letter box' and hiring a flat. The cover story she created was that she was going to Bristol as a woman writer collecting experiences of the Blitz from children for a BBC programme.

At every stage of the training, instructors wrote reports on the agents' progress and achievements, noting their particular strengths and weaknesses. These and a final overall report were sent to Maurice Buckmaster, who shared them with Vera Atkins, and then used them to assess the agents' readiness and decide which women should be sent into occupied France and in what role. As time went on, and the demand for agents to be sent into France in advance of the Allied invasion increased, training became more urgent and more rushed.

Coding and communication

Wireless was the main means of communication between agents in the field and SOE headquarters in London. Agents who returned to England often carried information and personal messages from other agents but wireless was the lifeline and the link between agents and SOE. All messages sent and received had to be in code. It was through coded messages that information was sent about the state of a circuit, about supplies being dropped in, where and when agents would be arriving or leaving, and so on. All agents learned basic coding but those who were to be sent into France as wireless operators had to go through specialist and very demanding training, even those who had

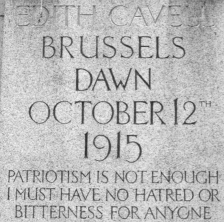

Edith Cavell.

Propaganda poster which exploited the execution of Nurse Edith Cavell by the Germans.

Detail from the memorial statue showing Edith Cavell's last words.

Edith Cavell's memorial statue, St Martin's Lane, London.

Mata Hari: 1906 image, wearing only breast covering and jewellery.

Mata Hari (1906 postcard).

Mata Hari: execution 1917 – probably a reconstruction, maybe around 1920.

'Kill that File' – chasing after a recalcitrant file in the Registry, 1919. The cartoon appeared in the programme for the *Hush Hush Review*, an MI5 review show, 1919.

Eager Girl Guides who worked as messengers for MI5 during the First World War. The image is taken from *Outbursts from Waterloo(se) House*, book of caricatures printed and privately circulated towards end of WWI. The original caption reads: 'The Electric Bells having broke, the G.G.'s (not Grenadier Guards) sit outside Maj. D.'s door in case he wants them.'

Violette Szabo. Imperial War Museum

Blue plaque on Violette Szabo's home, Burnley Road, London.
Thanks to Simon Adams

Stockwell children painted this mural of Violette Szabo in 2001.
Thanks to Simon Adams

Violette Szabo, bronze bust, Albert Embankment, London. Author's photo

In memory of SOE: detail from Violette Szabo memorial, London. Author's photo

Odette Sansom.
Imperial War Museum

Yvonne Cormeau.
Imperial War Museum

Noor Inayat Khan.
Imperial War Museum

Noor Inayat Khan.
Personal file HS 9/836/5 The National Archives

Madeleine Damerment.
With thanks to Madeleine Brooke for
permission to use

**Croix de Guerre, Légion d'honneur & Médaille de la
Résistance awarded to Madeleine Damerment.**
Thanks to Madeleine Brooke for permission to use

Letter from Vera Atkins to Madeleine Damerment's mother informing her that despite their ongoing efforts there was still no news of her daughter.

Thanks to Madeleine Brooke for permission to use

Room 238,
The War Office,
Hotel Victoria,
Northumberland Avenue.
London, W.C.2.

Any further communication on this
subject should be addressed to:—

Flt/O. V. M. ATKINS.

le 15 décembre, 1945.

Chère Madame,

Je regrette beaucoup de vous faire savoir que nous sommes toujours sans nouvelles de votre fille, Madeleine. Les recherches continuent et nous ne manquerons pas de vous faire savoir aussitôt que nous avons des nouvelles.

Je tiens à vous faire savoir que Madeleine a laissé un Testament qui se trouve entre les mains de notre Departement de Finance.

Veuillez croire, chère Madame, à mes sentiments distingues.

Madame Damerment,
Bureau des Postes,
Marquette,
LILLE, Nord.

1939   1945

IN HONOURED MEMORY OF THOSE MEMBERS OF THE
WOMEN'S TRANSPORT SERVICE (F·A·N·Y)
WHO GAVE THEIR LIVES FOR THEIR KING AND COUNTRY.

M.W.ANDERSON   M.DAMERMENT L.d.H C.d.G   M.L·M.Mc.KENZIE MILLIGAN E.G.SADLER
Y.E.M.BEEKMAN C.de.G. B.M.DICKIE   D.MORGAN   H.J.P.SALMON
D.BLOCH   B.E.EBDEN   R.E.NELSON   J.SHEPLEY
E.M.BOILEAU   M.HEATH-JONES   M.C.PEAKE   L.M.STALKER
A.BORREL   J.HILDICK-SMITH   E.S.PLEWMAN C.de.G.   E.P.STANGER
M.S.BUTLER   N.INYAT-KHAN G.C. B.E.RAMSAY   N.C.STAPYLTON
M.BYCK   C.LEFORT   F.L.RAWLINS   B.SWINBURNE-HANHAM
C.E.CLERK-RATTRAY V.E.LEIGH   L.V.ROLFE C.de.G. V.R.E.SZABO G.C.C.de.G.
C.D.CROOKE   C.M.LOPRESTI   D.H.ROWDEN C.de.G. M.J.THOMPSON
K.CROSS   D.M.MANNING   Y.RUDELLAT   P.C.WOOLLAN
     NEE PORTMAN   C.M.BRADFORD (IN JAPAN) 7-3-1947

W.T.S. (EAST AFRICA)

B.M.AUSTIN   B.DUNBAR THOMSON. B.KENTISH   M.SYKES
A.CALLISHER   W.GREY   F.F.MOOJEN   P.H.LE POER TRENCH
  H.C.CAMERER   S.HOOK   R.SOUTHEY

THEIR NAME LIVETH FOR EVERMORE.

WTS (FANY) Memorial, St Paul's Church, Knightsbridge.

With thanks to St Paul's Church, Knightsbridge.

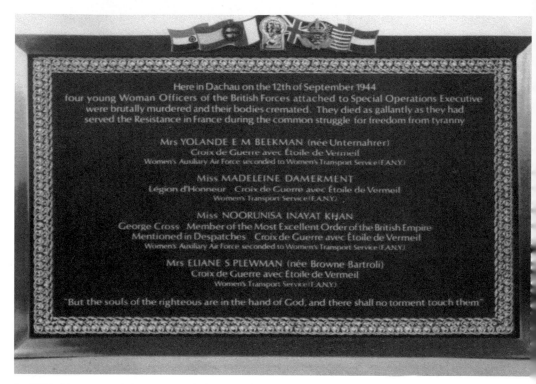

Here in Dachau on the 12th of September 1944
four young Woman Officers of the British Forces attached to Special Operations Executive
were brutally murdered and their bodies cremated. They died as gallantly as they had
served the Resistance in France during the common struggle for freedom from tyranny

Mrs YOLANDE E M BEEKMAN (née Unternahrer)
Croix de Guerre avec Étoile de Vermeil
Women's Auxiliary Air Force seconded to Women's Transport Service (F.A.N.Y.)

Miss MADELEINE DAMERMENT
Légion d'Honneur   Croix de Guerre avec Étoile de Vermeil
Women's Transport Service (F.A.N.Y.)

Miss NOORUNISA INAYAT KHAN
George Cross   Member of the Most Excellent Order of the British Empire
Mentioned in Despatches   Croix de Guerre avec Étoile de Vermeil
Women's Auxiliary Air Force seconded to Women's Transport Service (F.A.N.Y.)

Mrs ELIANE S PLEWMAN (née Browne-Bartroli)
Croix de Guerre avec Étoile de Vermeil
Women's Transport Service (F.A.N.Y.)

"But the souls of the righteous are in the hand of God, and there shall no torment touch them"

In 1976 this memorial was unveiled at Dachau in memory of the SOE women killed there:
Yolande Beekman, Noor Inayat Khan, Eliane Plewman, Madeleine Damerment.

Vera Atkins, intelligence
officer SOE French section.
From personal files, The National Archives
HS 9/59/2

already learned wireless operation in the WAAF.

The role of the wireless operator was absolutely crucial to the success of SOE operations and it was generally agreed to be the most dangerous role in the circuit. Wireless operators had to transmit and receive all their messages in code; they had to be able to translate messages into agreed codes, then transmit them by Morse code at a speed of about twenty-two words a minute. As well as transmitting the message, they also had to include special pre-arranged safety checks proving that they were genuine. These could be deliberate spelling mistakes or special words, agreed with London in advance. There were two types of security checks: 'bluff' checks, which could be revealed under torture and 'true' checks, which should never be revealed. The true checks were particularly important: if they were not included in a message, the probability was that the wireless operator had been captured. An agent's and indeed a circuit's safety could depend on coded clues within the messages being understood by the London HQ and any warnings about whether the agents were being watched or had been arrested were vital pieces of information: ignoring these warnings could have – and indeed did have – disastrous consequences. Agents developed their own individual style of transmitting, known in the jargon as their 'fist'; it was a type of Morse fingerprinting, and those who received the messages, usually FANYs working at the listening station at Grendon, soon came to recognize individual agents' transmissions. This itself could be a security check: if messages started coming in that were apparently from a known agent but not in his or her 'fist', it could mean that the agent had been arrested and German wireless operators were using the agent's wireless.

At different times, wireless operators used different code methods – Playfair, double transposition and the one-time pad, which was the most successful. Most agents used a poem as the basis for their coding system with each agent having his or her individual poem. It could be a poem that the agent knew well, or one that was written specifically for them. Agents who needed to improve their coding skills were sent to Leo Marks, the young, brilliant and somewhat idiosyncratic code-master of SOE. He was the son of Benjamin Marks, owner of the famous bookshop at 84 Charing Cross Road, immortalized in Helen Hanff's book of the same name. Marks never forgot how vulnerable agents were in the field, and did all in his power to improve coding systems, initiating the use of silk for carrying codes – as agents used various letters they could be cut off and destroyed, and the use of a one-time pad. He also encouraged the use of original poems rather than overworked poems, which he argued Germans listening in could break quickly because they were too familiar. Marks himself wrote many of the poems that agents used.

As well as learning how to code, wireless operators needed to know about atmospherics, wavelengths and jamming as well how to handle and hide their bulky equipment, which could weigh as much as 30lbs, and how to place and handle the aerial, which itself could be 70 feet long. Sometimes W/T operators had assistance but, given the dangers of the work, they often spent long periods on their own. It could be a lonely role.

A favourite spy

MOST SOE WOMEN agents were sent directly into France. Some were sent elsewhere, among them Krystyna Skarbek, better known as Christine Granville, the name she adopted when she worked for SOE. Christine Granville was an extraordinary and courageous woman. According to journalist Murray Davies of the Mirror Group, she was 'the first Bond girl', the prototype for Vesper Lynd in *Casino Royale*; apparently Winston Churchill described her as his 'favourite spy'. According to her SOE personal records held in The National Archives in London, the SOE considered her to be a 'person of remarkable courage and intelligence'. It is hardly surprising: Christine Granville may have been the prototype for a Bond girl but her real life exploits were far more extraordinary and thrilling than any fiction.

Christine Granville was born Krystyna Skarbek in or near Warsaw, Poland in 1908; her personal file gives her birth date as 1915 but subsequent researches have uncovered documents listing the earlier date. Her family was wealthy – her father, who claimed the title of count, was a bank official – and she enjoyed a privileged upbringing. She was a stunningly good-looking young woman, with a great love of adventure. She made an early, unsuccessful, marriage, but re-married in 1938, this time to Jerzy Gizycki, a diplomat who also enjoyed adventure. The two of them went to live in Addis Ababa, Ethiopia, when Gizycki was made Polish consul there.

In 1939 German forces invaded Poland: Krystyna and her husband left Ethiopia immediately for London where they arrived in October 1939. Jerzy offered his services as a spy for British intelligence and Krystyna volunteered to go into Poland to help gather information, distribute propaganda and help the Resistance movement. Initially there was some objection to her ideas but after a while SOE approved her plans. According to her SOE records held in The National Archives, on 7 December 1939:

> '4827 [Krystyna Gizycki] visited me. She is a very smart looking girl, simply dressed and aristocratic. She is a flaming Polish patriot. She made an excellent impression... Her idea is to bring out a propaganda leaflet in Buda and to smuggle it over the frontier herself. (She is an excellent skier and a great adventuress. She explained to me the route she would take. It appears that she has visited the Polish winter resort of Zakopane for many years and knows every man in the place. It was her chief delight at one time to help the boys smuggle tobacco over the frontier just for the fun of the thing. She is confident that these men will help her now). She is absolutely fearless herself and certainly makes that impression. She is able to get regular reports from the interior of Austria and Poland... She needs money for her work and I think she is going to earn it.'

Just a few days later, on 21 December, Krystyna set out for Hungary where she established her base. Within a very short time she had opened a route into Poland, initially persuading a slightly reluctant member of the Polish Olympic ski team to assist her in crossing the Tatra mountains and, before being forced to leave Hungary, crossed the Polish border six times and the Slovakian border eight times. On her journeys into Poland she carried sabotage material, secret mail and large sums of money, any of which, in the event of her arrest, might have 'seriously compromised her'. According to her records, on one occasion during the severe winter of 1940/1941 she walked for six days through a blizzard in temperatures as low as -30°C at times. More than a dozen Poles lost their lives in the region while trying to cross into Hungary.

During her time in the region, Krystyna met and formed a relationship with another agent, Andrzej Kowerski (known in SOE as Andrew Kennedy). She managed to organize the escape of British prisoners of war from Poland into adjacent neutral countries, and to gather important military and political information from Poland and Hungary, working with spies for the Polish Resistance, she assembled a dossier with photos of German troops massing on the borders of the Soviet Union, which at that time had signed a non-aggression pact with Germany. This intelligence provided clues that Germany was planning to invade the Soviet Union. She also worked with Resistance workers to carry out sabotage on communication lines on the main Danube route leading into Germany from Yugoslavia, Romania and Hungary. She was arrested twice, once in Slovakia and the second time in Hungary but each time managed to escape on her own initiative. During her second arrest and while being brutally interrogated, she bit her tongue hard enough to draw blood, coughed and managed to convince her questioners that she was suffering from tuberculosis. Fearing the illness, her questioners released her, together with Kowerski, and in May 1941 she was smuggled out of Hungary into Yugoslavia in the boot of a Chrysler car belonging to British ambassador Sir Owen O'Malley. Kowerski, who had been masquerading as a used car dealer, followed. From there the two made their way through Nazi-occupied territory to SOE headquarters in Cairo, Egypt. Along the way, Krystyna assisted the Polish Section in Istanbul as a courier until called to Cairo to carry out similar work in the Middle East, particularly in Syria.

Krystyna stayed in the Middle East until spring 1944; she was given a special course in subversive techniques, including parachute training, then in June 1944 was sent to North Africa to work with SOE's Algiers section. In July 1944, now using the code name Pauline Armand, she was parachuted into Southern France to help French Resistance fighters in advance of the American ground invasion of the area. She soon acquired a reputation for extreme bravery and quick thinking: on one occasion, German soldiers stopped her near the Italian border. She was told to put her hands in the air, which she did, revealing a grenade under each arm, pin withdrawn. The soldiers fled.

Possibly, however, her most famous exploit was the audacious rescue of her circuit chief, Francis Cammaerts, a former pacifist and one of the star agents of SOE's F section, who with two other British officers, had been arrested by the Gestapo in Digne in August 1944. According to Cammaerts' written account, which is in Christine Granville's file in The National Archives:

'We were arrested on the 13th August, and taken by the Gestapo to their headquarters and then to the barracks. Pauline [Christine Granville] spent three days and three nights trying to get together a *corps franc* who would attack the small German garrison at the barracks, and offered to lead them herself. The French Commandant of the FFI decided that the risk was too great, so she chose the last possible solution, knowing that we were to be shot on the night of the 17th, and went and interviewed the Gestapo herself, bluffing them with stories of the proximity of American troops, the imminence of heavy bombardments, the great importance attached by the Allies to our safety, and her own exalted relations, thus frightening certain of their lower ranks into cooperating in our escape. The way in which she handled these thugs… was unbelievably skilful. She took voluntarily one chance in a hundred, and undoubtedly if it had not come off she would have been shot with me.'

Krystyna's boldness paid off: the prisoners were woken up and, expecting to be executed, were in fact taken to a car where Krystyna was waiting.

As if this was not enough, during the same month Krystyna convinced some seventy Polish soldiers in the German army to desert. In a statement by Lieutenant Colonel Cammaerts about 'Christine Granville' dated 20 November 1945, he wrote:

'While Christine Granville was operating in the Col De Larche area, she obtained, by her own personal efforts, the surrender of the Larche garrison. Working entirely on her own she approached foreign elements in the German Army, particularly Polish troops, and persuaded them to steal all the arms of the garrison and surrender, carrying with them the breech-blocks of the heavier weapons. This work was of extreme danger. The Germans were fully aware that we were attempting this type of subversion and had taken every possible step to prevent it… The surrender of the Larche garrison seriously affected the German plans for an attack over the Col De Larche which might well have brought severe difficulties to the advancing American columns.'

Not surprisingly SOE recommended Krystyna Gizycki for an award on the grounds of 'her cool bravery and total disregard for her own safety' and she was awarded the British George Medal and the French Croix de Guerre. She was also appointed to the Order of the British Empire (OBE). Her life after the war however was difficult; she found it hard to settle to civilian life and for various reasons was unable to obtain British citizenship. She suffered from depression and in 1952 while working as a stewardess on an ocean liner, was murdered by one of the staff who had been stalking her.

Chapter 6

Behind Enemy Lines

'You had to be careful. You had to have eyes in the back of your head.'

YVONNE CORMEAU

O nce training was complete, and before agents departed, Buckmaster presented each agent with a gift – a gold cigarette case or cuff links for the men, and gold powder compacts for the women. They could be kept as souvenirs, or used as bribes or sold when in enemy territory. Then agents just had to wait until they were told that it was time for them to be sent into France. Typically agents spent the waiting time organizing their affairs, writing their wills and sometimes writing letters or cards to their families, which were left with Vera Atkins who posted them from whichever area women had said they were stationed. If asked to, Vera Atkins also from time to time sent what were known as 'good news' letters to agents' families: these said nothing about what the agent was actually doing but provided reassurance that the person was well. Most families had absolutely no idea that their relatives were actually operating in secret behind enemy lines; Madeleine Damerment's family, for instance, knowing that she had escaped from occupied France believed she was safe in England, perhaps working for a naval officer's family. They did not find out until much later that she was an SOE agent who had returned to France in 1944. Many women too spent the waiting period rehearsing their cover stories to ensure that they were word and cover perfect.

Moonlight drops
There were two ways of getting into France: by sea or by air. In the early part of the war agents were taken by boat from Falmouth to Northern France, or, if they needed to be dropped in Southern France, were flown to Gibraltar and from there travelled by sea on a felucca

to the Riviera coast, which is how Odette Sansom travelled to France. Most agents however were dropped into France by air, either parachuting in, or being landed. Probably around 1,000 agents were sent into France by parachute, which carried its own risks; there was always the danger of landing in a tree, on a building, or straight into the arms of waiting French or German police. However, if all went well a reception committee would be waiting to meet the agent, who would be hurried off to a safe house. Yvonne Cormeau was parachuted into France as a radio operator on 28 August 1943.

'On a Sunday afternoon I was taken to a house not far from the airfield and given a wonderful meal. I thought at the time it was the condemned man's last meal. I was… dressed up in my jump suit. Then I went into the aircraft… We took off in a beautiful sunset… I was given a nice hot drink by the despatcher and then… he opened a hole in the floor of the fuselage. He… attached my silk cord to the side of the aircraft and told me to get ready… I knew when the green light came on and the despatcher gave me a sign, I had to fly through the hole… The slipstream from the motors carried me off. Slowly but surely my 'chute opened and I didn't even feel the jerk on my shoulders… it wasn't a long drop. I took off my jumpsuit immediately and handed it to the French people who were meeting me. I only had a handbag, with my money in it, which was strapped behind my back, cushioning the lower vertebrae of the spine… I was dressed in what I thought was normal for France: black coat and a skirt with a silk blouse and black shoes.'

Initially SOE suffered a severe shortage of air transport for their agents: the RAF was very resistant to the idea of being used for special duties – not wanting to spare their planes and also because the higher echelons were unhappy about the whole set up. Eventually however two special duties squadrons were formed: Squadron 138 which used Whitley, Halifax and Stirling aircraft to drop agents and supplies, and Squadron 161 which used Lysander and Hudson aircraft to land and pick up agents. The Lysander was particularly suitable for the job. It was a small plane with a short flying range so only travelled to Northern France, operating out of a base at Tangmere, Sussex, but it could be landed almost anywhere and in a small area. Pilots and navigators needed to be highly skilled: they had to fly below enemy radar, navigating by landmarks such as rivers, lakes, church steeples, railway lines and roads. Once they arrived at the landing spot, they touched down, agents left the plane by means of a small ladder attached to the plane, returning agents climbed aboard, and the pilot took off again. Usually the whole dropping operation only took a few minutes.

Dropping agents into France could only take place at the time of the full moon and the few days before and afterwards, so that pilots had maximum visibility. Even then there were sometimes clouds over the moon, or the weather was bad and flights had to be postponed, which could be rather nerve-wracking for waiting agents. Women were given very little time to prepare; once the conditions were thought to be right, they were told to get ready. Vera Atkins always made a point of going with the women to see them off, maybe having a meal with them the night before, and waving them off from the airdrome. Before leaving, women were given their false identity papers and went through a final check; buttons, pocket contents, clothing labels, jewellery – everything was thoroughly checked and double-checked. It was not unusual for agents to have forgotten to leave family photographs behind, or perhaps the stub of an English cinema ticket. Sometimes Vera Atkins gave the agent a packet of French cigarettes, or a French newspaper just to add to their cover. Finally, all agents were offered a so-called L tablet or cyanide pill in case of torture. Some agents had these sewn into their clothes.

Couriers
Despite all their training, nothing could entirely prepare women for the dangers and realities of operating undercover in Nazi-occupied territory. Being dropped into France was just the start of what was a very dangerous mission. Arriving in France was risky in itself: if all went well, agents were met by members of a circuit or local Resistance fighters and taken to a safe house. But there was always a strong possibility that plans had been leaked and French police or Germans could be waiting. Sometimes a safe house had been compromised, and newly-arrived agents found themselves having to sleep in the open, or make their way to a far more distant safe house. SOE could not, by definition, always have the most up to date information about conditions on the ground.

Once in occupied France, agents had to find somewhere safe to stay, perhaps a small hotel or pension – they were advised to keep away from large hotels which were usually swarming with Germans – or more permanent accommodation, such as an apartment or bedsit, which was safe and that they could use as a base. They had to spend time familiarizing themselves with the area they had been sent to and establish their cover story so that they could start building up information sources and contacts. Agents had to be constantly on their guard. As M.R.D. Foot has said, agents spent their working lives on a 'razor's edge of peril'. Towns were seething not just with German soldiers but also the French Milice, to say nothing of informers. Anybody could be listening at any time, whether in a café, restaurant, on a bus or train, or even just in the streets. Many French men and women were keen to help the Allied cause, joining the Resistance movements and helping SOE agents with safe houses, food and clothing, but there were also many informers. No agent could be complacent.

'...you never knew, wherever you were, in a train or a restaurant, if anybody was listening. An occupation is one of the most awful things because you're not at home. You have to be careful of everything.'

(Pearl Witherington)

One of the first women to be sent to France was Yvonne Rudellat. A Frenchwoman, she had been living in England since her teens, and was working as a receptionist in a London hotel when an SOE agent spotted her. She was married but separated. At 45, grey haired and with a fresh complexion, she was one of SOE's oldest female agents. According to her instructors, she was 'an intelligent and extremely sensible woman' with 'a cheerful and attractive personality'. Her instructors also stated that she gave a misleading impression of 'fluffiness', but considered that her 'air of innocence and anxiety to please should prove a most valuable "cover" asset.' It needed to be. Code-named Suzanne and with a cover name Jacqueline Gauthier, a widow from Brest, Yvonne Ruddellat left England on 21 July 1942, arriving in the South of France by boat on 30 July in a dreadful storm. She made her way north on her own, crossing the border into occupied France by hiding in the coal bunker of a steam engine. She arrived in Paris then went on to Tours where she worked as a courier with the *Prosper* circuit, which was to become SOE's largest network in France. By March 1943 Yvonne Rudellat had travelled hundreds of miles as a courier in the Loire district, delivering messages and carrying out dangerous liaison activities between the various groups in her circuit, providing information about aircraft drops of weapons and supplies. She travelled everywhere by bicycle, having to pass numerous enemy controls, sometimes with explosives hidden in a basket fixed to the handlebars. As well as being a courier, she took part in a sabotage operation of the Chaingy power station and personally blew up two locomotives in the goods station of Le Mans. An extremely brave woman, in June 1943, while waiting for a supply drop, she was caught by the Gestapo; she defended herself with her revolver but was shot and captured. She was eventually sent to Belsen concentration camp where she died of typhus days after the camp was liberated.

In September 1942, just two months after Yvonne Rudellat left England, another two women were dropped into France, this time by parachute. They were Frenchwoman Andrée Borrel, who had been involved with the French resistance before escaping and arriving in England in 1942, and who had been on the same training course as Yvonne Rudellat, and Mauritian-born Lisé de Baissac. They travelled together on the plane but separated as soon as they arrived in France, Borrel to work with the *Prosper* circuit as a courier, and de Baissac (code name Odile) to be a courier and liaison officer on the *Scientist* network but liaising with two other circuits: *Physician* (*Prosper*), which was led by Francis Suttill and the *Bricklayer* network, under France Antelme. Her mission was also to form a new circuit. Using two different cover stories – poor widow or amateur archaeologist – she completed two missions in France, gathering information about dropping zones and training resistance groups.

By 1943 there were at least eleven women operating behind enemy lines, and more followed as the need grew, particularly as plans for the Allied invasion of Normandy took shape. Most went as couriers, using varied cover stories: poor widows, travelling sales representatives, secretaries and an amateur archaeologist – anything that would enable them to travel around without arousing suspicion. Moving around occupied France was extremely risky and couriers often had to cover great distances on foot or by bicycle, carrying information, money or even explosives from one circuit or sub-circuit or another. If they were stopped – and they often were – they needed to be sure that their identity papers and cover stories held. Germans were not the only danger; agents also needed to keep a close eye out for the *Milice*, or French militia, a paramilitary force specially created to assist the Germans. Often agents had to travel by train, which was risky; many agents often found themselves sitting next to German soldiers. It was safer to travel by night but that brought its own discomforts. Pearl Witherington was sent into France in September 1943, as a courier. Code-named Marie, her cover was that she was a travelling sales representative for a cosmetics firm:

'The job of a courier was terribly, terribly, terribly tiring... We never wrote and we never phoned. Any messages were taken from A to B and the territory we were working on was really very big... apart from Paris we had Chateauroux, Montlucon, down to

Toulousee, from Toulouse to Tarbes, up to Poitiers. It meant mostly travelling by night and the trains were unheated. One of the jobs I did regularly was going from Toulouse to Riom near Clermont-Ferrand. I'd leave Toulouse at seven o'clock at night and get to Riom at eleven o'clock the next morning, absolutely frozen stiff… and having had nothing much to eat. Then I went into the safe house… where there was no heating either.'

It was extremely rare for a woman to actually run a circuit – men almost invariably did this job – but Pearl Witherington was an exception. Born in Paris in 1916 to British parents, she had been raised in France and was working with the British Embassy in Paris as assistant to the Air Attaché when the Germans arrived. With her mother and sisters, she escaped from occupied France and arrived in England in July 1941. She found work with the Air Ministry but wanted to do something that she considered more worthwhile; eventually her name came to the attention of SOE, and she was recruited. Her final training report stated that she was 'cool, resourceful and brave' and that 'although a woman, has got leader's qualities.' She was also considered to be probably the best shot – male or female – that the instructors had seen. From September 1943 until February 1944 she worked as a courier for *Stationer* network but in May 1944 her circuit leader Maurice Southgate was captured by the Germans and Pearl Witherington took over. With the coolness mentioned in her training report, she re-organized the circuit as well as organizing and supplying some 2,600 *maquisards* (French resistance fighters). On one occasion she and only forty *muquis* were attacked by 2,000 Germans; they put up a terrific fight in a battle which lasted fourteen hours. German losses were eighty-six and the *maquis* lost twenty-four men. Pearl managed to escape, hiding in a cornfield. Over the next few months she organized more than twenty air drops of weapons and supplies and led the *maquis* in various acts of sabotage on German communication lines. Following the war she was recommended for a military award but instead was awarded a civil award – the MBE. She refused it saying there was nothing civil about what she had done. She died in 2008 aged 93.

Pearl Witherington survived the war but many female agents did not. SOE sent thirty-nine women into France as special agents. They needed every ounce of what Selwyn Jepson had described as their 'cool and lonely courage' because thirteen never returned.

Other women who operated as couriers behind enemy lines included Nancy Wake, who acted as a courier for the French Resistance before joining SOE. She had lived an exciting double life under the noses of the Germans, living a respectable life by day married to a French businessman and helping Allied airmen to escape to safety by night. The Germans, who were a constant threat, nicknamed her 'White Mouse' and she eventually escaped to England where she joined the SOE and did sterling work in France, working with the Resistance in preparation for the Normandy landings. Other courageous couriers included Diana Rowden, who liaised between agents and resistants between Marseille, Lyon and Paris, Vera Leigh, who was also involved with the Resistance before joining SOE, and Violette Szabo.

Violette Szabo

Immortalized in the film *Carve Her Name with Pride* (1958), described by fellow agent Odette Sansom as 'the bravest of us all', and the subject of many books, Violette Szabo is known today as one of SOE's most famous female couriers. She was born Violette Reine Elizabeth Bushell in Paris on 26 June 1921. Her mother was French, a dressmaker, and her father was English. He did various jobs – working as a bus driver, selling used cars and as a storekeeper. The family spent time in both France and England but eventually settled in Burnley Road, Stockwell, London. Violette went to school in Brixton. She was very athletic and had a reputation for being something of a tomboy. She left school at the age of 14 and started working; when war broke out she was a sales assistant on the perfume counter in what was then the Bon Marché department store on the Brixton Road. With the Fall of France in 1940, Violette, like many women who had roots in France, felt she needed to contribute to the war effort and joined the Women's Land Army but only for a brief period. French men and women who had escaped from France were arriving in London and on 14 July – Bastille Day – the Free French held a parade in London. There she met Etienne Szabo and, after a rapid romance, they married in August. Days later Etienne was deployed to North Africa and Violette joined the Auxiliary Transport Service (ATS) but left when she discovered she was pregnant. Her daughter Tania was born in 1942, but Etienne was killed at the Battle of El Alamein, never having seen his daughter. Shocked and distraught, Violette was left a war widow with a very young child, uncertain what her next move should be.

At some point Violette received a letter from a Mr Potter asking her to come for an interview: she went for the interview but what she did not know at the time was that Mr Potter was actually Selwyn Jepson, chief recruiting office for SOE, who in their search for suitable recruits must have spotted Violette Szabo. Given her fluent French and her knowledge of the country she would have been exactly the sort of person to interest SOE. According to her biographer, Susan Ottaway, the actual details of how Violette was found and the details of her interview are uncertain, but during the second interview Violette eagerly volunteered, no doubt keen to play a role in bringing down the people she held responsible for her husband's death. She later told another agent, Frenchman Bob Maloubier, that she wanted to kill Germans. By July 1943 Violette had been security cleared and by September was going through SOE's intensive training course, learning demolition techniques, Morse coding, tradecraft and so on. She also went to Ringway for parachute training, spraining her ankle during her second jump, which delayed her departure for France. Her instructors' reports were ambivalent: there was some doubt that she had the right temperament for an agent in the field, she spoke French with an English accent, and it was also noted that she was concerned about her young daughter being looked after properly. Even so, it was decided to send Violette to France as a courier. Tania would stay with her grandmother. First though, Violette needed to improve her coding, which was causing difficulties and she was sent to see Leo Marks, SOE's chief cryptographer. He writes about their meeting in his book *Between Silk and Cyanide* and was obviously very taken by the young, rather striking woman in front of him. Each agent used a poem individual to them that they used for coding purposes, and it was clear that Violette was having difficulty with hers. It was a French nursery rhyme that she knew well, but she kept mis-spelling the words. Marks therefore presented her with a poem, *The Life that I Have*, which he had written following the death of his fiancée, who had been killed in a plane crash not long before. Violette loved the poem and immediately produced perfectly-coded messages. The following day she returned and gave him a chess set as a thank you gift. When Violette left the room, Marks had a strong feeling he would not see her again. He kept the chess set for many years, later giving it to a terminally sick child. Her code poem became one of the best-known poems of the Second World War.

Violette's first mission was to find

The Life That I Have

The life that I have
Is all that I have
And the life that I have
Is yours

The love that I have
Of the life that I have
Is yours and yours and yours

A sleep I shall have
A rest I shall have
Yet death will be but a pause

For the peace of my years
In the long green grass
Will be yours and yours and yours

(Leo Marks: code poem given to Violette Szabo. With thanks to The History Press for permission to reprint.)

out whatever she could about the *Salesman* circuit, which operated in the Rouen and Le Havre areas: its co-founder Philippe Liewer (code name Clémont) had arrived back in England and while he was there the circuit had been badly compromised: SOE needed up-to-date information. On 5 April 1944 Violette (code name Louise), using the identity Corinne Reine Leroy, a commercial secretary from Le Havre, was flown into France with Philippe Liewer. They were parachuted in and a reception committee met them and took them to a safe house. From there they went to Paris; it was too dangerous for Liewer to go to Rouen so Violette went on her own, travelling by train, surrounded by German soldiers. Once in Rouen, Violette established that the circuit had been seriously compromised: members of the circuit and resisters had been arrested, some had been tortured, and there were 'wanted' posters on the walls of some of the leading figures, including Philippe Liewer and Bob Maloubier. Violette removed one of the posters, which she took back to London. She also made a brief visit to Le Havre where she obtained valuable information about V1 sites on the Normandy coast. Armed with this information, Violette returned to Paris, did some clothes shopping in one of the smart department stores still operating, and together with Liewer, returned to England.

Violette spent a brief time in England catching up with her family and Tania, and then volunteered for a second mission: to return with Liewer to resurrect a *Salesman* circuit – *Salesman 2* – between Limoges and Pèrigeux in the Haute Vienne, south of networks formed by Pearl Witherington and others. On 8 June 1944, two days after the Normandy landings had begun, Violette, (now code-named Corinne) operating as Madame Villaret, the widow of an antique dealer, Liewer (now code-named 'Hamlet') and Maloubier were parachuted back into France, some kilometres south-east of Limoges. Members of the local *maquis* met them, they gathered up their supplies and parachutes and they were taken to a grocer shop in the village of Sussac where they spent the night. The local *maquis*, while enthusiastic, were poorly organized and it was decided that Violette, as courier, should make contact with another circuit leader Jacques Poirier (code name Nestor) some 50 km (31 miles) away. The following day Violette, armed with a Sten gun, set out with another agent, Jacques Dufour (code name Anastasie); they were travelling part of the way by car. According to Dufour's account, they arrived at a roadblock where German soldiers waved them to stop. Dufour stopped the car, he and Violette jumped out and started firing at the Germans, while at the same time retreating back through a wheat field. Violette urged Dufour to make good his escape, she continued firing but, after a brief while, was captured.

Violette was taken to the German headquarters in Limoges, where she was interrogated and tortured but revealed no information about the circuit. Her circuit made an attempt to rescue her but it was too late. On 16 June she was sent to Paris to Gestapo headquarters at the Avenue Foch, where she was tortured again. Once more she said nothing more and was sent to Fresnes Prison. On 8 August she was put on a train to Ravensbrück, together with other SOE agents who had also been captured, among them Lilian Rolfe, wireless operator with the *Historian* network, and Denise Bloch, who had worked with the *Clergyman* circuit. All of them were chained in pairs by their ankles. It was very hot and while they were on the train, there was an air raid. The train stopped and while their guards were absent, taking cover from the air raid, Violette and Denise crawled along the train getting water from the lavatory for other SOE prisoners, including a well-known agent Yeo-Thomas, who, despite appalling torture and imprisonment, survived the war and was able to give an account.

After harsh labour and punishment in various different camps, Violette Szabo, Lilian Rolfe and Denise Bloch, by now exhausted and suffering illness, were executed at Ravensbrück and their bodies cremated. Violette was aged just 23.

Violette Szabo was awarded the George Cross posthumously in 1946, the highest civilian award available. The citation was published in the *London Gazette*. The details were incorrect but nevertheless it stated that: 'Madame Szabo volunteered to undertake a particularly dangerous mission in France. She... undertook the task with enthusiasm... She was arrested and... atrociously tortured but never by word or deed gave away any of her acquaintances or told the enemy anything of any value. She was ultimately executed. Madame Szabo made a magnificent example of courage and steadfastness.' She was also awarded the French Croix de Guerre and the Médaille de la Resistance. In the 1950s, Dame Irene Ward mounted a campaign for Violette to be awarded the Victoria Cross, a military award, on the grounds that she had taken military action against the Germans, but there was opposition and it was unsuccessful. Dame Irene Ward remained convinced that this was because Violette was a woman. Since then there have been various films and books about Violette Szabo, including one by her daughter Tania, *Young, Brave and Beautiful* (2007). In 2008 a bronze bust of Violette Szabo was unveiled on the Albert Embankment, London.

Wireless operators

A number of women, including Denise Bloch, Patricia (Paddy) O'Sullivan, Lilian Rolfe, Noor Inayat Khan and Yvonne Cormeau were sent to France as wireless, or W/T (wireless telegraphy) operators. It was a hazardous job, considered by many to be the most dangerous mission of all in Nazi-occupied territory, and it was often very isolated. Because of the risks attached to wireless operators, they often worked separately from other members of the circuit, spending long hours or days alone hiding and waiting until it was time to send messages to SOE. Unless there was an emergency, all operators had to transmit at scheduled times, or 'skeds'. Every message that agents sent to and received from SOE had to be transposed into code or cipher – each circuit had its own system – and then sent in Morse code. It was a laborious task.

Transmitting and receiving messages took time, which made the job very dangerous, particularly if transmitting in towns. The Germans constantly monitored all wireless wavelengths and it took their armed direction finders only twenty or thirty minutes to get within a metre or so of an operator. Relays of thirty clerks with cathode-ray tubes in the Gestapo headquarters in the Avenue Foch in Paris kept a constant watch on frequencies and when a new set started up, they were aware of it immediately and were able to alert mobile direction finders. Agents were told to keep their transmissions as short as possible and to always keep on the move so they did not transmit from the same place but this was not always possible and many operators were picked up because they had stayed on the air too long or had transmitted from the same place too often.

One of the W/T operators captured in this way was Yolande Beekman (née Unternaharer). Born in Paris to a Swiss mother and a Dutch father, she was educated in Paris, London and Switzerland and had excellent language skills, although according to her instructors, spoke French with a slight Swiss accent. In 1941 she joined the WAAF and was trained as a wireless operator. SOE found and recruited her in 1943 and recommended her for training as an 'agent in the field'. She did her advanced wireless training alongside Yvonne Cormeau and Noor Inayat Khan. Described as having fair hair, blue-grey eyes and a fresh complexion, she was assessed by her instructors as having a 'quiet self-confidence and serenely cheerful outlook on life... She shows any amount of determination in mastering the intricacies of W/T.' According to her personal file in The National Archives, she was popular, had a good sense of humour and was very conscientious. One or two of the reports commented that she was 'not over-imaginative', and one particularly disparaging comment was that she was 'a nice girl... would make an excellent wife for an unimaginative man', which may well say something about that individual instructor's view of women. Either way it was generally considered that Yolande would make an excellent wireless operator. Her motive for volunteering for such dangerous work was 'idealism, the "good of the cause" and devotion to duty'.

Yolande was sent into France in September 1943 to work as a W/T operator for the *Musician* circuit in the Lille-Saint Quentin area; the circuit leader was a French-Canadian Gustav Bieler (code name Guy). She was landed in Tours and because the reception committee was unable to help her, she made her way, alone, to Lille via Paris, carrying her wireless equipment. For the next four months she worked closely with Bieler; as a result of her efficient and important transmissions at least twenty deliveries of weapons and other supplies were dropped into the area to be used by the resistance. Yolande herself often met the drops and helped to distribute supplies. While in the area Yolande stayed in various places, being put up by sympathetic French men and women but unfortunately ended up consistently transmitting from the same place – an attic above a chemist's shop where she stored her wireless equipment. She had to transmit three times a week at exactly the same time so it was not surprising that the German detector vans eventually tracked down her wireless signals and she was arrested, together with Bieler, in a café just outside Saint Quentin on or around 15 January 1944. She was taken to Gestapo headquarters at 84 Avenue Foch, Paris, then to Fresnes Prison, where other women – Odette Sansom, Diana Rowden, Noor Inayat Khan, Vera Leigh and Andrée Borrel – were also being held. From there she and others were taken to Karlsruhe. She was shot at Dachau on 13 September 1944 at the age of 32. She was posthumously awarded the Croix de Guerre.

If the process of transmission was not sufficiently dangerous in itself – SOE estimated that a wireless operator could stay free for no longer than six weeks – the transmitters themselves were heavy and bulky, particularly during the early years. They also had an extremely long aerial, which brought its own difficulties and agents had to tune in the sets before they could even begin to transmit.

Where possible operators tried to find safe hiding places for their sets, but when they were on the move it was necessary to carry them. There were many near misses: on one occasion Yvonne Cormeau, whose cover was that she was a district nurse, and another well-known SOE agent George Starr (code name Hilaire) whose cover story was that he was a tobacco inspector, were in a car that was stopped by Geman soldiers. Yvonne Cormeau had her wireless set with her:

'We were... told to get out of the car. Then they put us in a ditch with two soldiers. Both had a pistol, one in my back and one in

Hilaire's back. The *feldwebel* [sergeant] was telling somebody on the radio that he'd stopped a tobacco inspector and a woman, the woman had a district nurse's card on her, what was he to do with them? My perspiration was coming down and the flies were sticking in my perspiration and I couldn't move, because if I'd moved they would have shot me... Then the crackle came again... He came back... "Get in the car" – which we did at once... Suddenly he asked me what was in the case... which, of course, was my radio set. I opened it. I knelt on the seat and showed it to him. He asked me what it was. I said "Radio", which, in German, means X-ray as well as radio-set. In view of the fact that I was meant to be a district nurse, he thought it was an X-ray set. He said, "Go," and we got out very fast.'

Yvonne Cormeau had a number of narrow escapes, on one occasion being betrayed by a double agent; there were also 'wanted' posters displayed in the area where she was operating but she managed to evade capture, perhaps partly because she used car batteries rather than mains power, which may have helped her evade the detection finders. She operated for thirteen months in occupied France and transmitted more than 400 messages back to London, which was a record for the F section. She survived the war and was subsequently made an MBE and awarded the Légion d'honneur, the Croix de Guerre, and the Médaille de la Résistance.

Noor Inayat Khan
Noor Inayat Khan was one of SOE's most unlikely women agents – she was born of pacifist parents and herself was a very gentle, self-effacing and modest young woman, who opposed violence and duplicity. She was perhaps the last person one might have thought would volunteer for a dangerous for a job behind enemy lines, which, by definition involved both duplicity and violence. But she did. Interestingly, she was not the only pacifist to volunteer: Francis Cammaerts, one of F section's most outstanding agents, had not only been a pacifist before the war but also had applied for exemption as a conscientious objector until his brother was killed, and he felt he could no longer remain separate from the war effort and joined SOE.

Noor Inayat Khan was very different from most of SOE's other female agents; for a start she was an Muslim Asian woman with a royal background. She was born in Moscow on 1 January 1914, the eldest of four children. Her mother, Ora Ray Baker, was American of British parents and possibly a distant relative of Mary Baker Eddy, who founded the Christian Science movement. Her father, Inayat Khan, was Indian, a musician, a teacher and a Sufi, the great grandson of Tipu Sultan, the eighteenth century Muslim ruler of Mysore, who had been killed fighting the British. Not long after Noor's birth the family moved to London, where they lived in Gordon Square, then in 1920 moved to France, eventually settling in a house in Suresnes that had been bought for them by a Sufi benefactor. Noor's father named the house Fazal Manzil, or the House of Blessing. Noor's childhood was a happy one, full of music, dance and religion; her father was a well-respected Sufi teacher who taught his children the principles of honesty and non-violence. In 1927 Noor's father died and Noor took responsibility for the family as her grief-stricken mother was unable to cope. An academically gifted young woman and a keen musician, Noor wrote stories and poems and played the harp. She studied music at the *Ecole Normale de Musique* in Paris – one of her teachers was Nadia Boulanger – and went on to study child psychology at the Sorbonne. She continued writing, particularly writing stories for children and by the late 1930s was becoming an established children's writer. One of her books, *Twenty Jakata Tales*, was published in England in 1939. Her stories were also read on French and English radio.

When war broke out in September 1939 the family were still living in Paris; Noor, who loathed Nazism, did a Red Cross nursing course but by 4 June 1940 German forces were outside Paris. Despite their Sufi principles, which forbade killing, Noor and her elder brother Vilayat decided they should leave France for England to help the war effort in some way. Noor's other brother and his family stayed in France, intending to help the Resistance in the south, while Noor, her sister, Vilayat and their mother managed to get a boat out of France, arriving in Falmouth on 22 June 1940.

Once in England, Vilayat joined the Royal Navy working on minesweepers and Noor enlisted with the WAAF as a wireless operator. She also changed her name to Nora Baker in keeping with her new life in Britain. In 1942 SOE, having spotted Noor because of her fluent French and wireless skills, invited her for an interview. Like all the other recruits, she did not know why but thought she was going to the War Office. Selwyn Jepson interviewed her in November 1942. He was very impressed by Noor and made up his mind immediately that she was the right recruit for SOE; she was patient and security-minded and in his view would make an excellent wireless operator. Unusually, Jepson spelled out the nature and the dangers of the work during their first interview and Noor immediately volunteered. She was however concerned about her mother's well-being and how she would manage without her but in her formal letter of acceptance stated that she now thought her mother would get used to her absence, Noor would be able to provide some financial assistance for her, and that winning the war was in the end more important than family responsibilities.

Having been recruited into SOE and commissioned into the FANY, Noor embarked on her training in February 1943. Like other agents she was taught how to survive in enemy territory, how to use weapons and explosives and how to cope with interrogation and torture. She was also given further training in wireless telegraphy, codes, ciphers and Morse code. Her training reports were complementary, although she was described as being 'pretty scared of weapons', clumsy and lacking confidence. It was also said she 'hadn't the foggiest what the training was going to be about'. In March 1943 Lieutenant Colonel Gordon described her as 'a person for whom I have the greatest admiration. Completely self-effacing and unselfish... extremely modest, even humble and shy'. She was also extremely conscientious. In April Lieutenant Holland reported that she had 'thrown herself life and soul into the life of the school.' He described her as 'very feminine in character, very eager to please, very ready to adapt herself to the mood of the company, or the tone of the conversation, interested in personalities, capable of strong attachments, kind-hearted, emotional and imaginative' and went on to say that her motive for volunteering was idealism. 'She felt that she had come to a dead end as a WAAF, and was longing to do something more active in the prosecution of the war, something which would make more call on her capabilities and, perhaps demand more sacrifice.' Interestingly perhaps he also commented that Noor didn't 'appear to have any romantic ideas of the Mata Hari variety. In fact, she confesses that she would not like to do anything "two-faced", by which she means deliberately cultivating friendly relations with malice aforethought.'

Subsequent reports were more critical and as Noor neared the end of her training, most of her instructors had serious doubts. In May 1943 one report stated: 'Not over-burdened with brains but has worked hard and shown keenness, apart from dislike of the security side... She has an unstable and temperamental personality and it is very doubtful whether she is really suited for work in the field.' Buckmaster savagely underlined the statements, and wrote above them in pencil: 'Nonsense' and 'We don't want them over-burdened with brains'. He also wrote 'Makes me cross' on the bottom. Some instructors were clearly concerned about Noor's 'mystical' and idealistic upbringing and wondered if this might set up an emotional conflict for her. It was suggested that care be taken in the field that 'she not be given any task which set up a mental conflict with her idealism. This might render her unstable from our point of view.' Overall she was considered too emotional, rather exotic and not sufficiently security-minded.

Maybe the instructors were right; they certainly seem to have realized that Noor Inayat Khan was rather different from the other women. Even so, and despite these reservations, there was a desperate need for wireless operators and it was generally agreed that Noor was an excellent radio operator. Buckmaster decided she should be used and Noor was therefore told to prepare herself for a mission in France. The mission briefing, which was very detailed and included her various security checks, information about safe houses and so on, is still in her file at The National Archives in London. In a 2006 BBC documentary about Noor Inayat Khan, called *Princess Spy*, M.R.D. Foot was asked whether Noor should have been sent to France. He replied, 'How can I tell? I thank God it was never my responsibility.'

Before Noor left for France, however, she was sent to Leo Marks, SOE's code master, for some extra training in coding; her coding was apparently erratic. Just as he wrote about his meeting with Violette Szabo in his book *Between Silk and Cyanide*, so too Marks describes his meeting with Noor. Marks felt very responsible for the safety of agents and prepared himself for meeting Noor by reading not just her training reports but also her book *Twenty Jakata Tales*. According to his account, he was struck by Noor's extraordinary beauty and sensitivity, and found himself wondering what on earth she was doing in SOE, to the extent that he hoped she would fail his coding instruction and not be sent into the field. In the end, because he knew that Noor had been brought up never to tell a lie – which in itself was a concern for the instructors – he told her that if she coded incorrectly she would effectively be lying to him. Her coding improved.

On 16 June 1943, Noor (code name Madeleine and with the cover identity of Jeanne-Marie Renier, a children's nurse), together with another agent, Cecily Lefort, was flown by Lysander from Tangmere, Sussex, into a field in the Loire Valley. She was the first female wireless operator to be sent into France. A second Lysander left at the same time, carrying Diana Rowden. The agent who met Noor, Henri Déricourt, later proved to have been a double agent responsible for betraying a great many SOE agents. He was unable to help her with a safe house so travelling first by bicycle and then by train she made her own way to Paris. Her mission was to work as a wireless operator in the Le Mans region for Henri Garry, a locally recruited agent who headed the *Cinema* (later *Phono*) circuit, one of the sub-circuits of the *Prosper* network, which was headed by Francis Suttill.

Noor arrived in Paris, reached her safe house, began to meet circuit members and began transmitting to London within seventy-two hours of arriving in Paris; she had to use another agent's wireless because hers had been damaged on landing. However, it turned out that Noor had arrived at a very bad time: within a week or ten days of her reaching Paris the Gestapo arrested the whole of the *Prosper* network's inner circle: Andrée Borrel, Francis Suttill and Gilbert Norman. The *Prosper* circuit had grown too large and unwieldy, mistakes were being made, and agents themselves were not displaying as much security as they should: the initial three who were arrested regularly met together at the same café and restaurant and did not always speak in French. As the Germans uncovered more information, so the arrests continued, hundreds of local agents were rounded up and either shot or imprisoned, and a number of circuit leaders were also arrested. Some, such as Francis Antelme, managed to get out and back to England.

Noor narrowly escaped arrest and went into hiding, but after a while went back to a safe house in Paris, from where she continued transmitting to London. She was now the only SOE wireless operator in Paris, and in extreme danger. She was, of course, also the only remaining link between Paris and the SOE in London. Knowing about the collapse of *Prosper*, Buckmaster had instructed remaining agents to get out quickly but there is some uncertainty about what happened with Noor. According to most accounts, Buckmaster instructed Noor to come back to London but she refused, saying that she wanted to stay and rebuild the circuit. After the war the question of whether Buckmaster should have insisted that she return was hotly debated and it was also claimed, but not proved, that he had not actually recalled her. Either way, according to Colonel Gubbins, Noor's situation was now 'the principal and most dangerous post in France'.

Keeping constantly on the move, Noor continued to transmit, lugging her wireless with her, which was no small achievement. The set she carried weighed about 30lbs and she was a slight woman. Carrying such a heavy weight but making it look as if she was just carrying a small suitcase would have quite a feat. She had a number of narrow escapes; on one occasion two German officers stopped her and asked what was in the case; she told them it was a movie projector. On another occasion she enlisted the help of a young German soldier to loop her 70-foot long aerial onto the branches of a tree outside her room. She told him she wanted to listen to some dance music on the radio.

What neither Noor nor SOE knew was that the Germans had been listening into her transmissions for quite a considerable amount of time. Because of their listening equipment at the Avenue Foch, they knew when a new operator started transmitting and they knew that there was an operator, code-named Madeleine operating somewhere in Paris but they could not find her. Amazingly enough, she continued to transmit without being found for twelve weeks, twice the amount of time that any wireless operator was expected to survive. Noor would have known she was in danger but, no matter what her instructors' reports had said, she was pleased to be where she was: in August she transmitted a message to SOE asking for new radio equipment and also sent a handwritten note asking for a FANY-style white mac and thanking Baker Street for sending her to Paris saying, 'It is grand working with you. The best moments I have had yet.'

Eventually the Gestapo caught up with Noor on or around 12 October 1943, although she was betrayed rather than discovered. The sister of one of the people she was working with was jealous of her and betrayed her to the Germans for 100,000 francs. One evening when Noor returned to her flat, she found the Gestapo waiting for her: the flat was just round the corner from the Avenue Foch. According to some accounts, she put up a tremendous fight, so much so that one of the Gestapo threatened to shoot her, but eventually she was overpowered. On searching her flat, the Gestapo found a school notebook in which she had written down all her messages, in code and in plain language ('*en clair*'). Apparently she had misunderstood the instruction in her mission briefing to 'be extremely careful with the filing of your messages'; she thought this meant she had to keep her messages. Armed with this material and the information they already had about 'Madeleine', Noor was arrested, handcuffed and taken to the Gestapo's headquarters at Avenue Foch.

Other captured agents were already at the Avenue Foch, including Bob Starr and others from the *Prosper* circuit, who had been arrested in earlier round-ups. They were held in rooms on the top floor that had previously been servants' quarters but were now used as cells. Almost immediately Noor made her first escape attempt. Saying she wanted a bath, she managed to get out of the bathroom window onto the roof, but was caught. She was interrogated a number of times by Major Hans Kieffer, chief of the Paris Gestapo headquarters, who tried to win her trust, as he had done with a number of other agents, but she disclosed absolutely nothing. Interrogated after the war, Kieffer said that she was very brave and had told them nothing. In

'Madeleine, after her capture, showed great courage and we got no information whatsoever out of her.'

(Hans Kieffer, Commandant of the Paris Gestapo, deposition, 19 January 1947)

November 1943 Noor made a second escape attempt together with Bob Starr and another agent; they broke through the iron bars of their cell windows, got onto the roof and managed to get into a neighbouring apartment but were recaptured and Noor was sent to Germany. To all intents and purposes she just disappeared.

Back in London there was concern that Noor's transmissions had stopped and nothing had been heard from her. Eventually, in early October, a message came through saying that 'Madeleine' had had a 'serious accident and was in hospital'. The source of the information was someone called 'Sonya' but no one knew who she was and Buckmaster chose to ignore the possibility that 'hospital' meant prison. At around the same time the SOE began to receive messages that were apparently coming from Noor, although her security check had been omitted: this should have been a clear message to SOE that it was not Noor who was transmitting but again Buckmaster chose to ignore the implications. What had actually happened was that the Germans were using Noor's radio, together with all the information they had acquired from the messages she had recorded in her notebook to send messages to London in the hopes that London would reply sending valuable information. The signs were ignored – in fact new W/T equipment was sent following a request – and it would be several months before SOE finally accepted that Noor was missing; her set was still transmitting until February 1944 although she had by that time been taken away.

Noor Inayat Khan was executed at Dachau concentration camp on 13 September 1944, at the same time as Eliane Plewman, Madeleine Damerment and Yolande Beekman. After the war she was posthumously awarded the George Cross, only the third woman during the Second World War to receive such a prestigious award. To date only four British women have ever received it. However it was not until after the war that the full details of her final months and in fact of all the women agents labelled as 'missing believed prisoners of war', were actually known.

Chapter 7

Missing

'There now remains only the very slightest hope that your daughter may still be found alive.'
VERA ATKINS, LETTER TO YOLANDE BEEKMAN'S MOTHER, 22 DECEMBER 1944

The summer of 1943 had been disastrous for SOE's French section, with many agents betrayed and captured. Later it would be established that the Gestapo in Paris knew almost everything there was to know about F section – and the *Prosper* network in particular. After the war, and even before its end, information emerged, which proved that, working from their base at Avenue Foch, German wireless operators were playing a 'radio game' with London, using captured agents' radios and codes to continue sending transmissions and receiving valuable information, supplies and money in return. However as Allied plans for the invasion of Normandy advanced, there was increasing pressure on SOE to find, train up and send agents into France to arm and organize the Resistance to carry out sabotage in advance of the Allied troops. In February 1944 SOE sent a team of three into France. They were France Antelme (organizer of the *Bricklayer* network) a French-Mauritian and very experienced SOE agent who had already done two missions in occupied France and had managed to escape the *Prosper* round-ups, his wireless operator Lionel Lee and Madeleine Damerment (code name Martine) who was considered to be one of the best couriers available at that point and who was given the cover name Martine Jacqueline Duchateau.

Madeleine Damerment was a remarkable young woman from a courageous and patriotic background, which no doubt influenced her decision to join SOE. Photographs show her as an attractive, fresh-faced young woman. In many ways she and her family continued the tradition of local family-based Resistance networks which were a feature of networks like *La Dame Blanche* during the First World War. Madeleine was born in the Pas de Calais in 1917 and named after her mother, Madeleine. Her father, Charles Eugene, was head postmaster in Marquette, just outside Lille; her mother, Madeleine Louise (née Godin) according to Madeleine's niece – also named Madeleine after her aunt – was the driving force and 'fighter' of the family. Madeleine was the middle of three sisters; her eldest sister was Jeannine and Charline was the youngest. After doing well at school, Madeleine worked in the telephone service in Lille as a clerk. Well before she joined the SOE she had already been living a dangerous existence working with the French Resistance.

When war began in 1939, Jeannine was living in the South of France with her husband and a young baby, and Charline was sent to stay with them. Following the German occupation of France in 1940, Madeleine and her parents became actively involved in the French Resistance. Initially her mother helped by openly providing Allied prisoners of war with food and clothing, something that she forcefully persuaded the German guards to let her do, but subsequently and secretly her parents hid Allied airmen in their house. Madeleine, working with a Resistance network set up by Albert Guerisse, helped smuggle them to safety along an established escape route, escorting them to Marseilles and Toulouse from where the local organization sent them through Spain and back to England. On one occasion, Madeleine heard that the Gestapo were making enquiries about her so she thought it wise to escape into unoccupied France, where she stayed with her sister and a friend in Toulouse. Her family managed to smuggle letters through to her telling her she was no longer a suspect so Madeleine returned to Lille from where she continued with her Resistance activities. She also took her younger sister back with her to Lille; according to Madeleine's niece, 'she headed back up through France to go from Free France to occupied France across a minefield at night' and also, to Charline's surprise, hid for one night in a brothel in Paris. Charline was smuggled across the checkpoint in the boot of a doctor's car, 'the doctor had a practice that straddled the checkpoint and he was a very brave man. He was used to taking people the other way but on that occasion he had a teenager in the boot of his car. I don't know if my aunt normally went across in the boot of a car or varied the route, but on that occasion she walked across the border', mingling with a group of French workers. According to the family's accounts, Madeleine 'had not been a factory worker and she always liked to keep her hands beautifully manicured so apparently a German soldier took her hand and said "Oh mademoiselle". She took his hand and stroked it and said "I finish work at whatever" and she went through unchallenged. She was apparently very good looking.'

Sympathetic neighbours, who knew perfectly well what was going on, warned the family if Germans were on their way, so that any Allied airmen in the house were told to get out through the back garden and hide until it was safe for them to return. But eventually the family and the network were betrayed. According to Madeleine's niece, 'Inevitably, I suppose, they were eventually betrayed. My aunt was not in the house; they came for my grandparents and apparently a neighbour saw my aunt coming up the street and said, out of the side of their mouth "Don't go home"; she understood, turned around and went down her own escape route, out through Spain and on to England.' It was later established that the network had been betrayed by a Resistance worker named Harold Cole. Madeleine's parents were arrested and imprisoned. Her father was deported and later died in a German concentration camp, her mother spent the remainder of the war in Loos prison near Lille, only managing to escape deportation to Germany because the railway lines were bombed. After the war, Madeleine's mother was awarded the Légion d'honneur for her work with the Resistance. Madeleine's younger sister Charline also survived the war but was arrested and probably tortured by the Gestapo before being released.

Madeleine used the regular escape route to get out of France, travelling through Marseilles and Toulouse and arriving in Barcelona in March 1942. She reported to the British Consul and was taken to Madrid but subsequently arrested because her papers were not in order. She spent about two weeks in prison, experiencing 'extremely rough and degrading' treatment according to an SOE report and then in May was released. She reported to the British Embassy and finally arrived in England in June 1942, where she gave an account of her activities so far and volunteered to work for the SOE. According to the report, the work she had already done was 'very risky as she was constantly out in the streets with British airmen and prisoners of war and had she been caught... the death penalty would have been unavoidable.' Madeleine did not know exactly how many people she had helped to safety but said it was 'a very considerable number'. Her report said that she was 'extremely modest in her statements and looked upon the whole matter as something very natural. She said many Frenchwomen are willingly doing this sort of work every day.' It was hardly surprising that she volunteered to be an agent for SOE.

Like other agents, Madeleine went through the usual training course. The report on her paramilitary training said she was 'aggressive' in close combat, was a 'fair shot with a pistol', and very good at explosives and demolitions. She was also good and 'painstaking' at map reading. Her final report described her as 'quite intelligent, practical, shrewd, quick and resourceful. She has imagination and cunning', although the instructors felt she did not always work very hard. She was described as having a strong character and a vivacious personality but was also said to be temperamental at times and in need of 'careful handling'.

Given her previous experience with the Resistance in France, there can be little doubt that Madeleine would have been a first-class courier but in the event she did not get the opportunity. She was due to work with the *Bricklayer* circuit and on the night of 28 February 1944 she and the other two agents were parachuted into a field near the city of Chartres. Ignoring all signs to the contrary, Buckmaster had chosen to believe that Noor Inayat Khan was still at liberty and because transmissions were apparently coming through from her, the arrangements were made through her radio. However Noor had been arrested months before and the Germans were using her set and codes. When Madeleine and the other agents landed in France on 29 February 1944, the Gestapo were waiting for them and they were captured immediately. Madeleine was taken to Gestapo headquarters at the Avenue Foch and interrogated but refused to say anything. In May she was sent to prison in Germany. On 13 September 1944 she was shot at Dachau at the same time as Eliane Plewman and Yolande Beekman. She was 26 years old.

Even though all evidence pointed to the fact that SOE circuits had been penetrated, more agents were sent into France ahead of the D-Day landings, among them Violette Szabo, Yvonne Basedon, a 22-year-old wireless operator who was parachuted into France in March 1944 and 20-year-old Sonya Butt, who was sent into France as a courier shortly before the Normandy landing.

'She [Madeleine's mother] was very, very proud of her, very proud of her. I think up to a point she felt that she did what she had to do, that she did her duty.'

(Madeleine Brooke on her aunt, Madeleine Damerment.)

Early reports

Agents and Resistance fighters worked feverishly in the period before the Allied invasion, sabotaging railways lines and cutting German supply and communication links. The Allied invasion of France began on 6 June 1944 (D-Day); by 25 August Paris had been liberated and Allied forces were making their way south. The work of SOE's French section was over; 118 agents were missing – thirteen of them women – but at this stage and in the post-invasion confusion no one knew which agents had survived and which had not. Discovering the truth would take a long time and there were many problems and mistakes along the way.

In August 1944 Vera Atkins went to Paris and based herself at the Hotel Cecil hoping that F section agents might make their way there. The situation was extremely confused; information about the fate of SOE's agents was sporadic and vague, not made easier by the fact that General de Gaulle wanted to obliterate all references to SOE. He wanted SOE out of France, preferring instead to promote the idea that the French had liberated themselves, without help from SOE. Information about agents did begin to trickle through and as it did, Vera Atkins updated the file cards she kept on all her agents. In June news had come through that Violette Szabo, Odette Sansom and Yvonne Baseden had been arrested and jailed in France. SOE hoped that with the liberation of France, their captured agents would be found in the jails but this did not happen. The jails were empty and agents had been moved. Rumours flew around that they had been shot in France but there was no proof and Vera Atkins was doubtful. A few agents, among them Pearl Witheringon, arrived at the base in Paris to great rejoicing and Vera Atkins tracked down another one of her surviving agents, Lisé de Baissac who was in a Normandy village, posing as a poor widow. One of the first women to be sent to France – as a courier and liaison officer – she had helped to set up a new circuit and had managed to survive the war. Around this time, Vera also learned that another of her agents, Muriel Byck, who had been sent to France in April 1944 as a wireless operator, had died of meningitis.

Vera Atkins returned to London and information about agents began to reach her via letters sent to her or the War Office from people who had known agents in the field, who had sheltered them or shared prisons with them. She began to compile casualty reports listing agents' names, where they had last been seen, the nature of casualty, source of information and so on. Most of them are still in personal files in The National Archives. In September, Vera Atkins heard of Yolande Beekman's arrest from a woman named Mlle Gobeaux, who had worked in a pharmacy in St Quentin; Yolande had transmitted from the attic above. She had gone to the British Embassy in Paris with her information and also had provided a date for Yolande's arrest: 13 January 1944. Disturbingly, Mlle Gobeaux reported that Yolande

126

'Yolande was brought by four Gestapo to the pharmacy. Source stated that her face was very swollen and she had obviously been very badly treated.'

(Vera Atkins' interview with Mlle Gobeaux.)

showed signs of ill treatment and had been taken to Paris by the Gestapo. Vera also received news that another of her agents, Cecily Lefort, was imprisoned in somewhere called Ravensbrück.

In late September a bitter and angry but very detailed report came through from one of SOE's agents, Marcel Rousset, who had been captured and taken to the Gestapo headquarters at the Avenue Foch, Paris. The building, which was at 82-86 Avenue Foch, was where many of the captured F section agents were taken. It was on four floors and headed by Hans Kieffer, by all accounts a plausible Gestapo officer who managed to ingratiate himself with a number of the agents and by so doing gained their trust. From evidence that emerged after the war, captured agents were shocked to find out how much information Kieffer already had about their activities and in some cases were persuaded to provide more, thinking it might save lives. One agent who never trusted Kieffer was Noor Inayat Khan. Avenue Foch also contained a wireless section run by Dr Josef Goetz, a coding expert. Captured agents were interrogated and tortured on the third floor. Rousset provided first-hand information about the torture room and mentioned a number of agents whom he had seen either at the Avenue Foch or another Gestapo prison in Place des États Unis. In all he had seen about sixteen F section agents, including John ('Bob') Starr, Gilbert Norman and France Antelme. Rousset confirmed that the Gestapo at the Avenue Foch had considerable information about F section and was angry that Buckmaster and others had failed to recognize how deeply *Prosper* had been infiltrated and therefore how much the agents' safety had been compromised. Rousset confirmed that agents had been tortured and described how he, together with other agents, including a group of women from Fresnes prison, which was about 12 miles (19.3km) outside Paris, had been transported to Germany. Rousset himself had been imprisoned in Silesia but had managed to escape. The following month the British gained access to the Avenue Foch premises where they found a list of agents' names written on a wall by the agents themselves: among them were those of Diana Rowden and Nora Baker (Noor Inayat Khan).

Until this point Vera Atkins had continued to send the occasional so-called 'good news' letter to families of agents telling them that all was well but now she began to inform the families that their relatives were missing, believed to be prisoners of war. In 1945 as Allied troops pushed through Europe and began liberating the concentration camps, Vera Atkins determined that she had to discover the fate of her missing agents. With an ever-growing flood of refugees and prisoners of war, it was probable that those who had survived might not be found and she wanted lists of the agents' names published and circulated to the various branches of the armed forces, the Red Cross and any other relevant organisations. She encountered considerable opposition, partly because SOE still did not want to break their secrecy and also because they did not want to advertise the fact that they had sent women into German-occupied territories. However in April 1945 SOE finally agreed that their missing agents' names should be published and circulated. The horrors of the camps were emerging and evidence suggested that SOE agents had been taken to and killed in the concentration camps, some of them under Adolf Hitler's infamous *Nacht und Nebel* (Night and Fog) decree of 1941, namely that enemies of the state, including spies, should be made to disappear without trace.

As more details came in they were passed directly to Vera Atkins, who followed up every lead, sending urgent letters to the War Office, passing on any information that she had, and asking for further enquiries to be made so that she could have confirmation of details coming through to her. Families of the missing agents were also asking for information, and every request was passed to Vera Atkins, who checked and double-checked all facts. She also met with some of the relatives and passed on whatever details she had. In July 1944, for instance, she met with Vera Leigh's step-brother, who apparently knew that his step-sister had been sent to France, and told him that Vera was missing but that she 'had reason to believe that she was a prisoner'.

Liberating the camps
Russian forces had liberated the first concentration camps in Eastern Europe in 1944; from April 1945 British and American forces liberated concentration camps in Western Europe. The first to be liberated was Buchenwald, by American forces on 11 April 1945. Vera Atkins received early reports from the camp, which, backed up by a first-hand account from a Free French agent, Bernard Guillot, who had escaped the camp days before it was liberated, provided evidence that about seventeen male SOE agents had been shot or hanged at Buchenwald, among them two Canadians Frank

Pickersgill and John MacAlister. Guillot, like Rousset, also stated that there were women among a transport that had left Paris for Germany, although the date that Guillot mentioned was earlier than the one given by Rousset. Guillot was shown photographs and identified Denise Bloch as one of the women. He did not however know what had happened to the women.

On 15 April 1945, British forces liberated Bergen-Belsen and once again news of the atrocities that were uncovered flashed around the world. One of the women who survived was a Polish woman named Marie Moldenhawer, who had met a woman called Jacqueline Gauthier in Ravensbrück concentration camp and knew she had been sent to Belsen. Jacqueline Gauthier was Yvonne Rudellat, one of Vera's missing agents. The information reached Yvonne Rudellat's daughter, who in July 1945 wrote to SOE asking for more information. Vera Atkins immediately shot off letters to the Red Cross and the British army asking for more details saying that:

'This woman went to the field for us in July 1942 and was arrested in June 1943. We know that she was eventually transferred to Ravensbrück camp and I have today heard that she was transferred from there to the camp at Bergen-Belsen at the beginning of March, 1945. It is believed that she was still there in April. We have the greatest interest in recovering her, not only because she is one of our oldest and best women agents, but also because she may be able to throw some light on the *Prosper* mysteries.'

Interviewed many years later by the Imperial War Museum, Vera Atkins remembered the flood of information that came to her after the concentration camps were opened:

'After 8 May people started streaming back from concentration camps. You'd get their stories and it was from them that you'd hear what had happened to those who had not returned. When a person was arrested, you did not know what happened to them subsequently – therefore the information brought by the returning agents was more than interesting and more than harrowing.'

Vera continued to hope that Yvonne Rudellat might be found alive among the survivors at Belsen, but she was not. It later turned out she had died some days after the camp was liberated. In early July 1946 Vera Atkins took a statement from Renne Rosier, who had been a political prisoner in Ravensbrück where she met Yvonne Rudellat (known to her as Jacqueline Gauthier). The two of them left Ravensbrück on 28 February 1945 on a transport to Belsen. She said that at that time 'Mrs Ruddelat [sic] was not in bad health, she suffered occasionally from loss of memory, but she remained of good morale and she looked neither particularly drawn nor aged.' When they arrived at Belsen, Yvonne Rudellat contracted typhus and dysentery – there was a typhus epidemic at Belsen in January 1945 – and became 'very weak'. According to Mlle Rosier, Yvonne Rudellat was still alive when the camp was liberated, although 'very tired and ill' but 'she died either on the 23rd or 24th April 1945 from exhaustion and general weakness.' She was buried in a communal grave. The War Office issued a formal death certificate on 9 August 1946. It stated that 'having regard to such information as is available concerning Ensign Yvonne Claire Ruddelat [sic] Field Ambulance Nursing Yeomanry, it has been recorded by the War Office that Ensign Ruddelat [sic] died from exhaustion in the camp of Bergen-Belsen Germany on the 23rd or 24th day of April 1945.'

Ravensbrück
Liberated by the Soviet Red Army on 30 April 1945, Ravensbrück was a concentration camp in eastern Germany that had been built specifically for women. Intended initially to hold maybe 1,000-1,500 women, at different times during its notorious history it held 15,000-30,000 women. In all approximately 130,000 female prisoners were sent to Ravensbrück, many of them Jewish. As in all the concentration camps, conditions were abysmal: women were humiliated, starved, worked to death and executed; some were experimented on and sterilized. In May 1945 Vera Atkins received news that three of her female agents had survived Ravensbrück and were coming home. The women were Yvonne Baseden who came out of Ravensbrück with the Swedish Red Cross when the camp was liberated, Eileen Nearne, who managed to escape and Odette Sansom. Each of them had information about other women agents. Yvonne Baseden told Vera Atkins that she had been taken to Ravensbrück from a prison in Dijon but on the way they had stopped at a 'holding camp' where she saw Violette Szabo, Lilian Rolfe and Denise Bloch, who had been brought from Paris. The three women were sent to Ravensbrück; she was sent there a few days later and never saw them again but heard news of them. Eileen Nearne confirmed that she had been on the same work detail as the three women but was later transferred to a munitions factory and then to forced labour on the roads near Leipzig, from where she

managed to escape.

Vera Atkins also met with Odette Sansom, who told her of the conditions at Ravensbrück and how she had managed to escape but she also told her that when she was removed from the prison at Fresnes, she was taken to a civilian prison in Karlsruhe, on the French-German border, where she was kept for two months before being sent to Ravensbrück. She told Vera Atkins that she was taken to Karlsruhe with seven other SOE women; from photographs she identified six of them: Madeleine Damerment, Vera Leigh, Diana Rowden, Yolande Beekman, Andrée Borrel and Eliane Plewman. Odette Sansom was unable to identify the seventh woman.

From other sources Vera had been able to acquire information about another one of her agents – Cecily Lefort, who had also been in Ravensbrück. A keen sportswoman, Cecily Lefort was married to a French doctor. In 1941 she had joined the WAAF and was recruited by SOE in 1943 as a courier to work with the Francis Cammaerts' *Jockey* circuit. She was captured by the Gestapo in September 1943 and, having been held at the Avenue Foch, was sent to Ravensbrück. According to witnesses, she became gravely ill and was given a 'pink card' declaring her unfit to work. She was probably gassed in about February 1945.

Vera Atkins now had some information on nearly all of her missing women agents and had also acquired a lot of detail about the men. One name was proving elusive – that of Noor Inayat Khan; apart from her name on a wall at the Avenue Foch, there were no other tangible facts about what had happened to her.

Towards the end of 1945 Vera Atkins went to Germany to gather more information. She was by now a commissioned officer in the WAAF. It had taken a long time for her to get permission to make the trip but evidence of the atrocities that had taken place in the concentration camp and the scale of the Holocaust had led to the setting up of war crime trials at Nuremberg so that the chief architects of the Holocaust could be tried for crimes against humanity. Nazi leaders and those who had run or worked at concentration camps were now in prison, which would give Vera Atkins the opportunity to gather precise information about her agents. Families of agents were also pressing for answers; they felt they had waited much too long. Violette Szabo's father was raising the matter with his MP and other families were beginning their own enquiries. In addition, Vera had acquired very disturbing details about three or four women who had been killed and burned, possibly whilst they were still alive, in the crematorium at a concentration camp called Natzweiler. With SOE due to close down at the end of 1945, it was essential for Vera Atkins to go to Germany. Format letters were sent to agents' families telling them that SOE was due to close and that they should contact the War Office for further information.

Vera Atkins made an initial trip to Germany in December 1945 but it was unsuccessful. She went back in January 1946, this time funded by MI6 and attached to the war crimes unit. She had to produce a monthly report for Major Norman Mott who had formerly been part of SOE's security section and was now handling SOE matters while the office was closing down. She was given three months to carry out her investigation; it was later extended to six months. During her time in Germany, she travelled extensively and interviewed a considerable number of people, including prison and concentration camp guards in her efforts to establish once and for all what had happened to the still-missing agents. In March 1946 she was finally able to establish the fate of the three women agents last seen at Ravensbrück. The camp commandant, an SS man called Johann Schwarzhuber, was being held in custody, and Vera Atkins interviewed him: he confirmed that Violette Szabo, Lilian Rolfe and Denise Bloch had been taken away from the work camp at Königsberg, to the main camp at Ravensbrück where they were shot and their bodies cremated. According to the statement given to Vera Atkins, their names were among a list of names drawn up by the Gestapo in Berlin for execution. Vera passed the information to Mott and told him where he would find the next-of-kin information for the dead women. In her report to the families, Vera Atkins stressed that the women had remained cheerful to the end and had gone bravely to their deaths. There is no doubt the women had died bravely but accounts later given to the war crimes trial at Ravensbrück exposed the dreadful conditions that inmates had experienced. Among these were eyewitness accounts of Violette Szabo, Lilian Rolfe and Denise Bloch, who were described as being weak, emaciated and very ill before going to their deaths.

Natzweiler

One of Vera Atkins' priorities was to discover what had happened to the women allegedly burned alive at Natzweiler and she travelled widely in her search for information, effectively establishing and tracing the route they must have taken from imprisonment in Paris to their end in the concentration camp. The concentration camp at Natzweiler was situated in a lonely area in the Vosges Mountains in

Alsace, the only concentration camp to be built on French soil. It was, until 1944, one of the Nazis' best-kept secrets. Natzweiler was built to house male prisoners only and was used mainly to incarcerate members of Resistance groups from all over Europe and others actively working to overthrow the Nazi state. Prisoners were treated brutally: worked to death, abused, shot, hanged and starved. The aim was that these men should be made to 'disappear' under Hitler's 1941 *Nacht und Nebel* decree: there should be no record of the person, nor the way they were treated, nor how they were killed; they should literally disappear into the 'night and fog' without trace.

Following the Normandy landings in June 1944 and as Allied troops approached, the SS cleared the camp, sending the surviving prisoners on a death march to Dachau. French forces liberated the camp in November 1944 and the Supreme Headquarters Allied Expeditionary Force (SHAEF) sent a fact-finding team to the camp. One member of the team was Yurka Galitzine, a British officer of Russian origin. Despite the secrecy surrounding Natzweiler there were records and he put together a report listing the beatings, shootings, hangings and sadistic cruelty carried out on prisoners. He heard that British men had been in the camp, and that some women, who were described as well-dressed spies, had been taken to the camp, and presumably killed. His report was suppressed, but the following month, *New York Times* journalist Milton Bracker went to the camp and published an article about it. Galitzine also publicized his findings through the *Daily Express*.

Vera Atkins had already heard about Natzweiler before leaving for Germany and had met with Yurka Galitzine in England. He could not give her any names but he thought that the women had been brought from Karlsruhe to Natzweiler. He also knew that two British men had been in the camp and one of them, according to rumours, had sketched pictures of the women. The two British men were SOE agents, Robert Sheppard and Brian Stonehouse, who before the war had been a graphic designer for *Vogue* magazine. Both of the men had been captured in France and sent to Natzweiler. Amazingly they survived not only Natzweiler but also Dachau. Some days later, before leaving for Germany, Vera Atkins was sent the testimony of an eyewitness, a man called Franz Berg, who had worked in Natzweiler. It made harrowing reading. According to Berg's statement, he had been a waiter and had been imprisoned on many occasions for various offences. By 1942 he was working in the quarry at Natzweiler and in 1943 was working as a stoker in the camp crematorium. The man in charge of the crematorium was called Peter Straub.

In his testimony, Berg described that on one afternoon in July 1944 four women – two English and two French – were brought to the cells in the crematorium building. According to his account they 'were carrying suitcases and coats over their arms and I think one had a travelling rug... They were all placed in the same cell, but about 8 o'clock that evening they were placed in solitary confinement, each in a separate cell.' He was told to fire up the crematorium furnace to its maximum heat by 9.30 pm and then to disappear. 'Peter Straub... told me also that the doctor was going to come down and give some injections. I knew what this meant... I was still stoking the fire of the crematorium oven when Peter Straub came in, followed by the SS doctor (a *Hauptersumfuhrer*... who had come... from Auschwitz). The doctor in uniform chased me out of the furnace room.' Berg and his cellmates stayed in their cell but they could hear what was happening outside; one of the men, Georg Fuhrmann also caught glimpses of what was going on in the corridor outside. 'He whispered to me that "they" were bringing a woman along the corridor. We heard low voices in the next room and then the noise of a body being dragged along the floor, and Fuhrmann whispered to me that he could see people dragging something on the floor... At the same time... we heard the noise of heavy breathing and low groaning... the next two women were also seen by Fuhrmann, and again we heard the same noises and regular groans as the insensible women were dragged away. The fourth, however, resisted in the corridor. I heard her say *"Pourquoi"* and I heard a voice which I recognized as that of the doctor who was in civilian clothes say *"pour typhus"*. We then heard the noise of a struggle and the muffled cries of the woman... I heard this woman being dragged away too... From the noise of the crematorium oven doors which I heard, I can state definitely that in each case the groaning women were placed immediately in the crematorium oven.' When all was quiet, the men left their cell and looked inside the crematorium oven where they saw four blackened bodies.

Berg was shown photographs: he recognized one of the women as Vera Leigh, who had been sent to France in 1943 as a courier with the *Inventor* circuit. He believed that one of the other women was Noor Inayat Khan. He said a third was dark haired and fatter than the others. Later, a prisoner who had managed to speak to the women told Berg they had come from Karlsruhe.

Before leaving England, Vera Atkins also heard from Brian

Stonehouse, who now remembered that while he was in Natzweiler he had seen some English 'girls' enter the camp in July 1944 and walk past him to the crematorium. He thought there were three women but not only had he seen them, he had also done quick sketches of two of them. Interviewed by the Imperial War Museum after the war, Brian Stonehouse said:

> 'They were all rather pale, in civilian clothes. You never saw any women in the camp and I couldn't understand what they were doing there. They hadn't make-up on but you could tell they'd been in jail for several months. One of the girls had a ribbon in her hair, a sort of defiant gesture... One of the girls had a fur coat on her arm; later on, one of the SS guards walked back up the camp with the fur coat over his arm... From an inmate's point of view they looked in good condition... They were executed that evening... I didn't know any of them but I made a description of them as soon as I got back.'

Brian Stonehouse also said that the young woman with a ribbon in her hair looked very English; Vera Atkins knew immediately that this had to be Diana Rowden, who always wore a ribbon in her hair and who although she had spent many years in France, and spoke French fluently, had a distinctively English appearance. Brian Stonehouse described the second woman, who was carrying the fur coat as smaller, with dyed blond hair through which dark roots could be seen, and Jewish in appearance. Vera Atkins did not recognize the description but began to convince herself that it may have been Noor Inayat Khan.

Once Vera Atkins arrived in Germany, and armed with the information Odette Sansom had given her about the women she had seen, she went to Karlsruhe prison to clarify exactly which women had been held there, for how long, when they left and where they were sent. She interviewed the prison warder, Theresia Becker, who had been warder of the women's prison for more than twenty years. She was shown photographs and stated that seven of them – Madeleine Damerment, Vera Leigh, Diana Rowden, Yolande Beekman, Andrée Borrel, Eliane Plewman and Odette Sansom – had arrived at Karlsruhe in about May 1944; they had been sent away in July 1944. The only name that she could remember was 'Martine', which was Madeleine Damerment's alias. She also commented that 'Martine' had arrived carrying a New Testament; Madeleine Damerment was a very devout Catholic. Vera Atkins also interviewed a number of other witnesses, among them a young

German woman, Hedwig Muller, who had also been in the prison and had become friendly with Madeleine Damerment, who she knew as 'Martine'. She confirmed that Eliane Plewman was also at Karlsruhe. Subsequently Vera Atkins was able to confirm that Yolande Beekman was there too.

By March 1946, having interviewed many witnesses and having amassed a considerable amount of details from various sources, Vera Atkins knew that eight women had been held at Karlsruhe and that they had left the prison in two separate transports, four of them in July 1944 and another four in September 1944. The first transport had been sent to Natzweiler: based on information she had received, Vera Atkins was certain that three of the women who went to Natzweiler were Vera Leigh, Andrée Borrel and Diana Rowden but she was still not certain about the identity of the fourth, who had been described as Jewish in appearance. By a process of elimination, she felt this had to have been Noor Inayat Khan but there were still doubts. In April 1946 she interviewed Franz Berg, who had stoked the crematorium at Natzweiler and took him in detail through the testimony he had already provided; he confirmed the fact that one woman had resisted and had been put alive into the crematorium. Following the interview, Vera Atkins was convinced that the fourth woman was Noor Inayat Khan. Accordingly she sent a report of her findings to Norman Mott in London, stating that as a result of her investigations she could confirm that on 6 July 1944 four of the SOE women had been executed by lethal injection at Natzweiler and their bodies cremated. She asked him to make arrangements to inform the next of kin so that the families of Vera Leigh, Diana Rowden, Andrée Borrel and Noor Inayat Khan could be informed of their deaths. Obviously any suggestion that they had been alive when put into the crematorium furnace was omitted; families were told that the women had been injected with phenol and cremated.

Two weeks later Vera Atkins attended the Natzweiler war crimes trial and gave evidence. She visited the camp and went into the crematorium, checking and confirming the details that she already had. During the trial, there was an attempt by senior SS staff to deny the fact that the four women had been in the camp on 6 July 1944 but, despite the secrecy which was supposed to surround Natzweiler, there were hundreds of witnesses who saw the women arrive. It was a men-only camp, so the arrival of four women was an exceptional circumstance. Hundreds of men saw them arrive and walk down a long slope that led from the barracks to the crematorium. A number of survivors gave evidence to that effect. Rumours had spread around the camp and two Belgian doctors, George Boogaerts and Albert Guérisse, who had been active in the Resistance, managed to exchange a few hasty words with the women. Guérisse had recognised Andrée Borrel from the Resistance. Evidence from survivors helped to establish the timing of events; men were told to go into their barracks at about 8.00 pm, which was unusually early, and to keep the windows closed and shuttered or curtained. Despite these precautions, all the men knew what was to happen and many said how helpless they felt. Evidence at the trial from Berg and medical orderlies confirmed the sequence of events: that the women had been brought out of their cells, that they had been injected with phenol and that they had been cremated. Evidence was also given that one woman had struggled and had scratched Peter Straub's face. Straub stated that the woman had shouted 'Vive la France'. Prisoners outside saw flames coming out of the crematorium chimney and knew the women had been executed. It was later believed that the woman who struggled was Andrée Borrel.

To all intents and purposes the fate of these four women was now known but even at that point information was coming through to suggest that the fourth woman was not Noor Inayat Khan; the prison records for Karlsruhe were discovered and there was no record of Noor having been there. Instead there was a name that Vera Atkins did not know, namely Sonia Olschanezky. Born in Germany the daughter of a Russian Jew, and a professional dancer, Sonia had been a member of the French Resistance and was recruited in France by SOE to join the *Prosper* circuit, which she did in 1943. She managed to avoid the *Prosper* round-up but was captured in January 1944 and imprisoned at Fresnes then taken to Karlsruhe. Because Sonia Olschanezky had been recruited for the SOE in France, Vera Atkins had never met her and knew nothing about her. She had assumed that any descriptions she was given of the fourth woman at Natzweiler had to refer to Noor Inayat Khan. But she was wrong. It was Sonia Olschanezky who was killed at Natzweiler, not Noor Inayat Khan. However, the official records were not changed at that point, so Noor's family, who were devastated by the news, believed Noor had died at Natzweiler.

Dachau
Following the Natzweiler trial, Vera Atkins focused on the other women who had been in Karlsruhe and who had left the prison in September 1944. Talking to many witnesses, Vera established that the local Gestapo had collected Madeleine Damerment, Eliane

Plewman and Yolande Beekman from Karlsruhe on 11 September 1944. Madeleine Damerment had taken a small case with her. Getting more information was difficult; many senior Gestapo had gone into hiding but Vera Atkins put out inquiries and eventually by May 1946 she was sent information obtained from a member of the Gestapo, Christian Ott, which stated that Madeleine Damerment, Yolande Beekman and Eliane Plewman had been sent to Dachau, a concentration camp in Bavaria, about 12 miles north of Munich. However, he also mentioned a fourth woman, who had been held at Pforzheim prison and joined the other three before they were taken to Dachau. The officer in charge of their transport was a man called Max Wassmer. According to Ott's evidence, the women were handcuffed and taken by train first to Munich and from there to Dachau. He was told they would be executed. According to his statement, the women were aged between 24 and 32 and well dressed. He said that one of the prisoners spoke good German and that on questioning them he found out that two of the women were English, one was French and the fourth was Dutch through marriage. One of the women told him she had been parachuted into France and had worked for the secret service. Ott and Wessmer took the women to Dachau, arriving at about 10.00 pm. Ott never saw the women again but according to his statement, Wessmer was present when the four women were executed and told Ott about it. According to Wassmer's account, as given by Ott, at about 8.30 in the morning the women were brought out of the barracks and told they were going to be shot. One of the women asked for a priest but her request was refused and she was told there was no priest in the camp. The four women were told to kneel down; apparently the two Englishwomen held hands, as did the other two women and all four were shot in the back of the head. Their bodies were taken away, presumably cremated. Ott did not know any of the women's names but he remembered that the German-speaking woman had a full figure and a pale round face: it was Madeleine Damerment.

Vera Atkins managed to track down Wassmer, who had been interned, and he confirmed the information. Once again Vera Atkins sent her report to Norman Mott. She also wrote draft letters for the next of kin. By and large the letters followed a formula and are all contained in the personal files at The National Archives. Vera Atkins did, however, amend the letter to Madeleine's Damerment's mother so that she should not know that her daughter arrived in France only to be arrested immediately by the Gestapo. Madeleine Brooke is the keeper of her aunt's papers, medals and surviving memorabilia;

138

among these is the letter sent to her grandmother telling her there was still no news of Madeleine and a copy of the letter that Norman Mott sent to Mme Damerment informing her of Madeleine's death.

Vera Atkin's report, which she sent to Major Mott on 25 June 1946, was headed:

SUBJECT: Mrs E.S. Plewman (FANY)
                 Miss Madeleine Damerment Alias Dussautoy, FANY
                 Mrs Y.E.M. Beekman, née Unternahrer

It has now been established that the above named were executed in the camp of Dachau in the early hours of 13 September 1944, probably by shooting. The full circumstances of this case are not yet known but the fact that they were killed in the early hours of 13 September 1944 has been definitely established. I assume that you will take the usual casualty action.

The facts, as far as they are known, are as follows:

Elaine Plewman was captured at Marseilles on or about 23 March 1944. It is believed that she passed through the prison of Les Beaumettes in Marseilles and was then sent to Fresnes near Paris. Yolande Beekman captured near St Quentin on or about 15 January 1944 and she was first taken to 84 Avenue Foch, Paris and later transferred to Fresnes. Madeleine Damerment was captured on landing on 29 February 1944 near Chartres. I believe she was taken to Fresnes straight away.

On 12 May 1944 they left Fresnes Prison together with Odette Sansom – who has returned safely – and Diana Rowden, Nora Inayat Khan, Vera Leigh, and Andrée Borrel who were killed at Natzweiler on 6 July 44. They went straight to Karlsruhe where they were put into the civilian jail for women where they remained until the early hours of 12 September 1944. I have seen the following witnesses apart from Mrs Odette Sansom in connection with their stay in Karlsruhe:-

Frau Becker and Fraulein Hager, in charge of the womens' [sic] jail, Karlsruhe as well as the three temporary wardresses all of whom remember the girls. I have also seen:

Fraulein Hedwig Muller… who shared a cell with Madeleine Damerment whom she knew as Martine Dussautoy. I enclose a letter from Hedwig Muller which she asks should be forwarded to Martine's mother. I also saw

Frau Else Sauer of 3 Nachtdgallernweg… Karlsruhe, who was in Martine's cell the night that she was fetched away. I attach Frau Sauer's sworn statement. From this it will be seen that she also knew Eliane Plewman by sight and that she saw her leaving at the name time as Martine. I also saw Frau Hagon... who shared a cell with Yolande Beekman. I attach translation of her deposition.

Whilst in the Karlsruhe prison the girls were not ill-treated; they were put into separate cells which they shared with one or two German prisoners – most of them appear to have been political rather than criminal prisoners – and there is no doubt that Hedwig Muller, Elise Sauer and Nina Hagen struck up a very real friendship with our girls and that they did everything possible to help them by sharing their food parcels and having their laundry washed, etc. Nevertheless they had, obviously, a very hard time of it and they became very anxious when first the four girls and then Odette Sansom disappeared and they could find out nothing about their fate. They were locked up in their cells during the heavy raids on Karlsruhe and apparently showed amazing courage and cheered up their cell-mates, all of whom spoke of them with the greatest admiration.

On the afternoon of 11 September, Frau Becker received instructions to prepare the girls for departure early next morning and she went round to each of the cells and returned to the girls their personal belongings and told them they would be moving off the next day. At about 1.30 am on 12 September they were called out of their cells by an elderly male warder who was on night duty and were taken down to the reception rooms where they were collected by Gestapo officers. I have interrogated various members of the Karlsruhe Gestapo and in particular the two officials who accompanied the girls to Dachau. Their accounts of the journey differ in several respects but I am satisfied that, in broad outline, the following took place:-

The girls were driven by car, accompanied by 3 Gestapo officials, two of whom have been identified as Kriminalsecretar *Wassmer and Ott, to the station of Karlsruhe or of the nearby town of Bruchsal and caught the early train for Munich, arriving in the later afternoon. Here they changed trains and caught the last train to Dachau, some 20 miles north-west of Munich. They arrived after dark and had to walk up to the camp which they reached about midnight. They were handed over to some camp official and spent the night in the cells. Between 8 and 10 the next morning (13 September) they were taken to the crematorium compound and shot through the head and immediately cremated.*

Vera Atkins attached translations of statements made by Max

Wassmer and extracts from Christian Ott's statement. Both men were in US custody and she was intending to interrogate them when they were moved into the British zone. She also asked Mott to send letters to the next of kin, and to the Mother Superior of a Catholic Convent where Madeleine Damerment had stayed whilst in England.

On 10 July 1946, Mott wrote to Madeleine Damerment's mother saying that it was 'with deepest regret that I have to inform you that your daughter, Madeleine, was killed in the early hours of 13 September 1944 in the camp of Dachau. According to what is believed to be a reliable report she was shot through the back of the head at close range and death was immediate. The body was cremated.' He went on to say that Madeleine had 'volunteered to return to France on a special mission in the company of two British officers when she was captured on 29 February 1944 near Chartres.' He explained that she been taken with seven other British women to Karlsruhe, which held various political prisoners, many of whom had been interviewed and one of whom, Fraulein Hedwig Muller, who shared Madeleine's cell, had befriended her. No doubt, in order to soften the blow, he then wrote 'whilst the long months spent in prison in Karlsruhe were certainly hard, I am glad to say that the girls were in no way ill-treated. The news of the Invasion and the Allied advance buoyed up their morale and they never lost their courage or their faith… I know this tragic news will be a great shock to you and the only consolation I feel able to offer is that until the end she was cheerful and of good faith and that while perhaps suffering equal hardship she was spared the horrors of a concentration camp. Madeleine worked and sacrificed her life for the Allied cause and this will not be forgotten by all who knew her both here and in France.'

An identical letter was sent to the Mother Superior of the French Convent in Hitchin, with whom Madeleine had become very close. She had left two wristwatches with the Mother Superior for safekeeping. Similar letters were sent to the families of all the women agents who were killed, although the more shocking details of their deaths were left out.

Chapter 8

Setting The Record Straight

'They died as gallantly as they had served the Resistance in France during the common struggle for freedom from tyranny.'
DACHAU, PLAQUE IN MEMORY OF SOE WOMEN

T he news of the women's deaths and the work they had been involved in came as a great shock to their families. While family members including Noor Inayat Khan's brother and Vera Leigh's stepbrother had guessed their sisters were involved in something very dangerous, others had no idea at all. Madeleine Damerment's mother thought her daughter was safe in England and, until she died until a few years ago, Madeleine's sister Charline, found it very distressing to talk about. Madeleine Damerment's niece also says to this day she finds it hard to read about the activities of the French Resistance. Other families too were devastated, among them Noor Inayat Khan's mother who was inconsolable, so much so that Noor's brother, Vilayat, subsequently wrote to Vera Atkins asking that any further information about his sister should be sent directly to him, not his mother. However, in the case of Noor Inayat Khan, the information given to the family that she had died in Natzweiler was wrong.

When Vera Atkins returned to England she interviewed Dr Goetz, who had masterminded the radio deception at the Avenue Foch; he had been taken to England for interrogation. He mentioned a female prisoner called 'Madeleine' – Noor Inayat Khan's alias – who had refused to co-operate in any way and confirmed that they had used her wireless and codes to deceive SOE. He also stated that she had been sent to Germany soon after being captured in 1943. In November 1946 Vera Atkins was forwarded a letter from woman called Yolande Lagrave, which had been sent to Lord Walkden, a Labour peer, and then sent to her. The writer, a Frenchwoman, had

142

been arrested by the Gestapo and sent to Pforzheim as a political prisoner. She was the only one of her group of prisoners who had managed to survive. She was repatriated in May 1945 and after the war had gone in search of a woman, whom she knew as Nora Baker. She wrote to Lord Walkden, whom she had known before the war:

> 'At Pforzheim where I lived in a cell, I was able to correspond with an English lady parachutist, who was interned there and who was very unhappy. Hands and feet chained, she was never allowed out, and I could hear the blows she received. She left Pforzheim in September 1944, but before she left she was able to let me know – not her name, that was too risky – but her pseudonym and this by means of her mess tin. I also registered the address "Nora Baker", Radio Centre, Officers Service, RAF.'

Nora Baker was the English name that Noor Inayat Khan had taken when she was in the WAAF. If she had been in Pforzheim in September 1944 she could not have been executed at Natzweiler in July. Confronted with this new evidence, Vera Atkins returned to Germany to find out more. While Vera Atkins was discovering new information about Noor Inayat Khan, so too was Vilayat Khan, who had also received a letter from Yolande Lagrave. From various accounts it emerged that Noor Inayat Khan had indeed been taken to Pforzheim where, considered by the Germans to be a very dangerous woman, she was singled out for 'special treatment', kept on near-starvation rations and regularly beaten up. She had managed to communicate with Yolande Lagrave and other French women prisoners by scratching messages on the bottom of her food bowl and they had done similarly. Her final message to them was 'I am leaving', which is when, as other evidence showed, she was taken to Dachau, where she was one of the four women executed there on 13 September 1944.

In July 1947 Norman Mott finally wrote to Vilayat Khan with confirmation that Noor Inayat Khan, after spending about two months at the Avenue Foch, had been imprisoned in Pforzheim jail and then taken to Dachau where she was executed. For Noor Inayat Khan's family this second blow was completely devastating; her mother never recovered. Vera Atkins now knew for certain that it was Sonia Olschanezky who had been killed at Natzweiler, but for some extraordinary and unknown reason she did not tell Sonia's family about her death. Perhaps ironically, it also later emerged that it was Sonia who had transmitted the message to SOE telling them that 'Madeleine' (Noor Inayat Khan) was in hospital, that is that she had been captured.

The reality of how the women were treated at Dachau was also glossed over; in fact the actual details were not known for many years. Instead the comforting image of the four women holding hands and being shot cleanly in the head remained the official story for a very long time. Even today, anyone who calls up any of the four women's names on Wikipedia is likely to find that version of events. However, as years went by the truth began to emerge. After the war a woman called Jean Overton Fuller, who had been a close friend of Noor, began to do her own research, travelling extensively through Europe to do so. She wrote up her findings in a book in a book about Noor Inayat Khan called *Madeleine*, which was published in 1952. Some while afterwards she received a letter from a Lieutenant Colonel Wickey who had worked for Canadian intelligence during the war. During this time he had met a German officer who had spent time at Dachau and who described Noor as looking 'much like a Creole'. From him he had learned details of Noor's last day at Dachau and they were harrowing. From his evidence, and other sources, it would seem that all the women were beaten when they arrived at Dachau but Noor was singled out for particularly appalling treatment. She was stripped and systematically abused and kicked in her cell throughout the night. The following morning, by now what one writer described as 'a bloody mess', she was beaten again and then shot in the head. It seems her last word was *'Liberté'*.

Recognition

After the war it took a while for the public to learn about SOE and its work. As news filtered through there was considerable debate about what it had achieved, and whether it had been appropriate to send not just women, but also what many people considered to be amateurs into enemy-occupied territory, where so many of them died. Not surprisingly SOE defended its record – there is little doubt that certain acts of sabotage were immensely important in France and elsewhere, and that SOE played a major role providing arms and supplies to resistance movements in various countries, as well as providing training and encouragement. The American General Dwight Eisenhower considered that the SOE's work had shortened the war by at least six months. At the same time, in Britain, there were demands to know what had gone wrong, particularly in France with the collapse of the *Prosper* circuit. Conspiracy theorists had a field day the must challenging theory being that Maurice Buckmaster had deliberately sent agents into France knowing that networks had been blown, which was hotly denied. As arguments and counter-arguments raged, there were demands from various people, including Dame Irene Ward, to set the record straight and let the public have the full story of SOE. Eventually, historian M.R.D. Foot – who had himself been dropped into France in 1944 – was asked to write an official history; he was given access to SOE files and his book *SOE in France* was published in 1966. Since then there have been many books on SOE, an organization which continues to fascinate the public. Some arguments continue, among them the question of whether Noor Inayat Khan should ever have been sent to France. The opening of SOE files in The National Archives since the late 1990s has also prompted more books about the SOE, particularly books on female agents who by and large have been overlooked, or at least not allocated nearly the same amount of coverage in books about SOE as the men, which given that SOE treated men and women equally, is perhaps odd.

The realization that women agents had been sent into France captured the public imagination, and a raft of films and books appeared during the post-war years, some highly sensational, some well-researched. The best-known films included *Odette* (1950), which told the story of Odette Sansom and *Carve Her Name with Pride* (1958), based on the life of Violette Szabo. There were the books by Jean Overton Fuller and one agent, Anne-Marie Walters wrote her account *Moondrop to Gascony* immediately after the war.

Even before the war was over Maurice Buckmaster was drafting recommendations for the women agents to be given official recognition of their bravery and contribution to the work of resistance in Nazi-occupied France. Three of the women – Odette Sansom, Violette Szabo and Noor Inayat Khan – were awarded the George Cross, the last two posthumously. Others received MBEs and George Medals. Madeleine Damerment, Andrée Borrel and others, as well as some of the British women agents were awarded the Croix de Guerre, Légion d'honneur and the Médaille de la Résistance. In May 1948, under the banner headline 'Brave Women Honoured', *The Times* announced the unveiling of a tablet at St Paul's Church, Knightsbridge, London commemorating fifty-two members of the FANY who had lost their lives during the Second World War, among them were women of the SOE. Yvonne Basedon, Vera Atkins, Odette Sansom and Violette Szabo's then five-year-old daughter Tania were present at the ceremony.

Wider recognition of women's role in SOE was a long time coming. It was not until 1976 that a memorial to the women who died at Dachau was unveiled. A small plaque had been placed in the Natzweiler crematorium the previous year, and in 1993 Odette Sansom (later Hallowes) unveiled a plaque at Ravensbrück in memory of Violette Szabo, Lilian Rolfe, Denise Bloch and Cecily Lefort. There are memorials and statues in France, and the Imperial War Museum in London contains a permanent exhibition on The Secret War, which displays information and memorabilia about the female agents, including Noor Inayat Khan's pistol. The public today perhaps only knows a few 'big names'; in 2010 author Shrabani Basu, who believes that Noor Inayat Khan has been seriously overlooked, founded the Noor Inayat Khan Memorial Trust to raise money for a statue of Noor to stand in Gordon Square, London. It will be the first statue to an Asian woman in London.

Active or passive
Today we probably know as much of the truth as there is to be known about how the women of SOE met their ends, although research never stops and new information may yet come to light. Immediately after the war there was something of an outcry about the fact that women had been sent to France as undercover agents, but that denigrates the choices that the women made. Female spies are often presented as sexual vamps or passive dupes; in 1915 Hamil Grant stated that women were incapable of being good spies because they could not be impersonal and were too inclined to be distracted by romantic involvements, but none of these views apply to the women of SOE. To a great extent their activities are in a continuing tradition of other women, in other times, who have also resisted occupation by an enemy and have done so covertly; there is a thread that connects the women of the SOE and the resistants of *La Dame Blanche*, who were patriots and brave women in the same way as the SOE agents.

It could perhaps be argued that the women were exploited; that those who sent them out knew they were unlikely to come back – it has been also been suggested that Buckmaster deliberately kept Noor Inayat Khan in Paris in an attempt to convince the listening Germans that the SOE did not know that their agents had been captured – a sort of radio double bluff. It may or may not be true – and both Buckmaster and Vera Atkins were disgusted by the suggestion – but that view belittles the commitment of these brave women.

Whether or not they were exploited; the women described in within the chapters of this book were volunteers. They made a conscious decision to undertake these dangerous missions, and had few illusions about what the outcome might be. Reading their official citations is very moving; the focus in all of them is on their courage and patriotism, as it should be. It could be argued that to some extent this emphasis reflects the imagery surrounding Edith Cavell and might suggest that the women martyred themselves, but nothing could be further from the truth. The women of SOE did not see themselves as martyrs nor were they passive victims any more than the women of *La Dame Blanche*; a direct contradiction of Hamil Grant's jaded view. They were committed, idealistic, thoughtful, patriotic and brave, and they single-mindedly risked their lives to fight against oppression and Nazism. Madeleine Brooke, who is named after an aunt she never met, considers Madeleine Damerment to have been a very special and 'absolutely remarkable' person. The same could be said of all the women of the Special Operations Executive.

Appendix

SOE women agents with F section, France
SOE sent thirty-nine women from England to France. One agent, Sonya Olschanezky, was recruited in France and did not go to Britain for training.

NOOR INAYAT KHAN ('Madeleine')
Wireless operator, *Cinema* sub-circuit
Flown to France night 16 June 1943
Captured on or around 12 October 1943
Executed Dachau 13 Sept 1944
Posthumous George Cross, Croix de Guerre

YOLANDE BEEKMAN ('Mariette')
Wireless operator, *Musician* circuit
Flown to France 18/19 September 1943
Captured 12/13 January 1944
Executed Dachau 13 September 1944
Posthumous Croix de Guerre

MADELEINE DAMERMENT ('Martine')
Courier, *Bricklayer* circuit
Parachuted into France 28/29 February 1944
Captured on landing 29 February 1944
Executed Dachau 13 September 1944
Posthumous Légion d'honneur, Croix de Guerre, Médaille de la Résistance

ELIANE PLEWMAN ('Gaby')
Courier, *Monk* circuit
Parachuted into France 13 August 1943
Captured Marseilles on or about 23 March 1944
Executed Dachau 13 September 1944

ANDRÉE BORREL ('Denise')
Courier, *Prosper* circuit
Parachuted into France night 25 September 1942
Captured 22/23 June 1943
Executed Natzweiler July 1944
Posthumous Croix de Guerre

VERA LEIGH ('Simone')
Courier/liaison officer, *Inventor* network
Flown to France 14 May 1943
Captured 30 October 1943
Executed Nazweiller July 1944

SONYA OLSCHANEZKY ('Tania')
Courier, *Juggler* network
Recruited in France, 1942
Captured 22 January 1944
Executed Nazweiler July 1944

DIANA ROWDEN ('Paulette')
Courier, *Acrobat* network
Flown to France 16/17 June 1943
Captured 18 November 1943
Executed Nazweiller July 1944
Poshumous MBE, Croix de Guerre

DENISE BLOCH ('Ambroise')
Courier & wireless operator, *Clergyman* network
Flown to France 2/3 March 1944
Captured 18 June 1944
Executed Ravensbrück January 1945
Posthumous Croix de Guerre, Légion d'honneur, Médaille de la Résistance

LILIAN ROLFE ('Nadine')
Wireless operator, *Historian* network
Flown to France 6 April 1944
Captured 31 July 1944
Executed Ravensbrück 27 January 1945
Posthumous Croix de Guerre

VIOLETTE SZABO ('Louise', 'Corinne')
Courier, *Salesman* network
Parachuted into France 5 April 1944, 8 June 1944
Captured 10 June 1944
Executed Ravensbrück 27 January 1945
Posthumous George Cross, Croix de Guerre, Médaille de la Résistance

CECILY LEFORT ('Alice')
Courier, *Jockey* network
Parachuted into France 16/17 June 1943
Captured 15 September 1943
Executed Ravensbrück February 1945
Posthumous Croix de Guerre

YVONNE RUDELLAT ('Jacqueline')
Courier, *Monkeypuzzle* network
Arrived France 30 July 1942
Captured 21 June 1943
Died of typhus Belsen 23 or 24 April 1945
MBE, Croix de Guerre

JULIENNE AISNER ('Claire')
Courier, *Farrier* network
Originally recruited in France, went to England
Flown to France 18 May 1943
Survived the war

FRANCINE AGAZARIAN ('Marguerite')
Courier, *Prosper* network [married to W/T operator Jack Agazarian]
Flown into France 18 March 1943
Returned England 17 June 1943

YVONNE BASEDEN ('Odette')
Wireless operator, *Scholar* network
Parachuted into France 18/19 March 1944
Captured 26 June 1944
Liberated from Ravensbrück, April 1945
Survived the war

SONYA BUTT ('Blanche')
Courier, *Headmaster* circuit
Parachuted into France 28 May 1944
Returned to England October 1944
MBE

MURIEL BYCK ('Violette')
Wireless operator, *Ventriloquist* network
Parachuted into France 9 April 1944
Died of meningitis in France 23 May 1944

MARIE-THERESE LE CHENE ('Adele')
Courier, propaganda distribution, *Plane* circuit
[needs more dates]
Survived the war

BLANCHE CHARLET ('Christianne')
Courier, *Ventriloquist* circuit
Arrived France by felucca 1 September 1942
Arrested October 1942. Escaped from Castres prison 16 September 1943
Brought back to England April 1944
MBE

YVONNE CORMEAU ('Annette')
Wireless operator, *Wheelwright* circuit
Parachuted into France 28 August 1943
Returned to England 23 September 1944
MBE, Légion d'honneur, Croix de Guerre, Médaille de la Résistance

LISE DE BAISSAC ('Odile', 'Marguerite')
Courier and organizer, *Artist* & *Scientist* networks
Parachuted into France 25 September 1942
Flown into France 9/10 April 1944
Survived the war
MBE, Légion d'honneur

YVONNE FONTAINE ('Mimi')
Courier, *Tinker* network
Resistant, worked with SOE in France, sent to England for training
March 1943
Returned France March 1944
Returned England 16 September 1944
Not commissioned into FANY so not considered by Vera Atkins to be
an official SOE agent

CHRISTINE GRANVILLE ('Pauline')
Courier, *Jockey* circuit
SOE missions in Hungary and Egypt

Parachuted into France 7 July 1944
Demobilised Cairo, May 1945
OBE

VIRGINIA HALL ('Marie', 'Diane')
Courier and organizer, *Heckler* network, also worked for OSS (Office of Strategic Services, US equivalent to SOE)
Sent to Vichy France August 1941
Joined US Office of Strategic Services (OSS) March 1944 and sent to France again
Distinguished Service Cross

MARY HERBERT ('Claudine')
Courier, *Scientist* circuit
Arrived France by felucca 31 October 1942
Arrested 18 February 1944; imprisoned but released after some months

GINETTE JULLIAN ('Adèle')
Wireless operator, *Permit* network
Parachuted into France 7 June 1944
Returned to Britain 22 September 1944

MARGUERITE KNIGHT ('Nicole')
Courier, *Donkeyman* circuit
Parachuted into France 6 May 1944
Returned to Britain around 12 September 1944

PHYLLIS LATOUR ('Geneviève')
Wireless operator, *Scientist* circuit
Parachuted into France 1 May 1944
Returned to Britain August 1944

MADELEINE LAVIGNE ('Mariette')
Courier, *Silversmith* circuit
Worked with SOE in France, trained in England, parachuted into France 23 May 1944
Died suddenly of embolism, Paris 24 February 1945
King's Medal for Courage in the Cause of Freedom

EILEEN NEARNE ('Rose')
Wireless operator, *Wizard* network

Flown to France 3 March 1944
Captured 25 July 1944
Survived Ravensbrück, transferred to labour camp Silesia
Escaped labour camp 13 April 1945
Returned to Britain June 1945
Croix de Guerre, MBE

JACQUELINE NEARNE (aka Josette Norville)
Courier, *Stationer* network
Parachuted into France 25 January 1943
Returned Britain April 1944
MBE

PATRICIA (PADDY) O'SULLIVAN ('Josette')
Wireless operator, *Fireman* network
Parachuted into France 23 March 1944
Returned to England 5 October 1944
MBE

ELISABETH REYNOLDS (aka Devereux-Rochester) ('Elizabeth')
Courier, *Marksman* circuit
Flown into France 18 October 1943
Arrested 20 March 1944
Interned Vittel but released during Allied advance

ODETTE SANSOM ('Lise')
Courier, *Spindle* network
Arrived France by felucca 31 October 1942
Captured 16 April 1943
Survived Ravensbrück; returned to Britain April 1945
George Cross, MBE, Légion d'honneur

NANCY WAKE ('Helene')
Courier, *Freelance*, also leader Maquis
Resistant in France until 1943, escaped to Britain
Parachuted into France 29/30 April 1944
Returned to Britain 16 October 1944
Croix de Guerre, George Medal, US Presidential Medal of Freedom,
Médaille de la Résistance

ANNE-MARIE WALTERS ('Colette')
Courier, *Wheelwright* network

Parachuted into France 3/4 January 1944
Returned Britain August 1944

ODETTE WILEN ('Sophie')
Wireless operator, *Stationer* & *Labourer* circuits
Parachuted into France 11 April 1944
Returned to Britain August 1944

PEARL WITHERINGTON ('Marie', 'Pauline')
Leader and courier, *Stationer* circuit
Parachuted into France 23 September 1943
Returned to Britain September 1944
Légion d'honneur, CBE, rejected civilian MBE

Archive References

Chapter 5: Special Operations Executive
p. 79 Vera Atkins: IWM Sound Archive 9551
p. 83 Gwendoline Lees: IWM Sound Archive 11087
p. 83-4 Odette Brown: IWM Sound Archive 26370
p. 87 Vera Atkins: IWM Sound Archive 9551
p. 90 Capt. Selwyn Jepson: IWM Sound Archive 9331
p. 91, 95 Yvonne Cormeau IWM Sound Archive 7369
p. 97 SOE training: The National Archives KV4/172
p. 98 ff Christine Granville: The National Archives HS/9/612

Chapter 6: Behind Enemy Lines
p. 103 Yvonne Cormeau: IWM Sound Archive 7369
p. 105, 106-7 Pearl Witherington: IWM Sound Archive 10447; *Guardian* obituary, 1 April 2008
p. 105 Yvonne Rudellat: The National Archives HS 9/1289/7
p. 112 Yolande Beekman: The National Archives HS 9/114/2
p. 113-4 Yvonne Cormeau: IWM Sound Archive 7369
p. 116 Noor Inayat Khan: The National Archives HS 9/836/5

Chapter 7: Missing
p. 124 Madeleine Damerment: The National Archives HS 9/1654
p. 126 Yolande Beekman: The National Archives HS 9/1142
p. 128-9 Yvonne Rudellat: The National Archives HS 9/1289/7
p. 128 Vera Atkins: IWM Sound Archive 9551, 18594
p. 133 Berg deposition: Vera Leigh personal file, The National Archives HS 9/910/3
p. 134 Brian Stonehouse: IWM Sound Archive 9852
p. 138-40 Madeleine Damerment: The National Archives HS 9/1654

Chapter 8: Setting The Record Straight
p. 142 Noor Inayat Khan: The National Archives HS 9/836/5

Bibliography

Bailey, Roderick in association with the Imperial War Museum, *Forgotten Voices of the Secret War: An Inside Story of Special Operations During the Second World War*, Ebury Press, 2008

Binney, Marcus, *The Women Who Lived for Danger: The Women Agents of the SOE in the Second World War*, Hodden & Stoughton, 2002

Crowdy, Terry, *The Enemy Within: A History of Espionage*, Osprey Publishing, 2006

Escott, Beryl E., *The Heroines of SOE F Section*, The History Press, 2010

Everitt, Nicholas, *British Secret Service During the Great War*, London Hutchinson, 1920 (eBook)

Foot, M.R.D, *SOE The Special Operations Executive 1940-1946*, Pimlico, 1999

Grant, Hamil, *Spies and Secret Service: The Story of Espionage, its Main Systems and Chief Exponents*, Frederick Stokes, 1915 (eBook)

Grayzel, Susan R., *Women and the First World War*, Pearson Education Ltd, 2002

Harris, Carol, *Women at War: In Uniform 1939-1945*, Sutton Publishing, 2003

Helm, Sarah, *A Life in Secrets: The Story of Vera Atkins and the Lost Agents of SOE*, Abacus, 2006

Hollis, Patricia, *Women in Public; The Women's Movement 1850-1900*, George Allen & Unwin, 1979

Knightly, Phillip, *The Second Oldest Profession: Spies and Spying in the Twentieth Century*, W.W. Norton & Co., 1987

Landau, Captain Henry, *Secrets of the White Lady*, G.P. Putnam's Sons, 1935

Mahoney, M.H., *Women in Espionage: A Biographical Dictionary*, ABC-CLIO, Inc, 1993

Marlow, Joyce, editor, *The Virago Book of Women and the Great War*, Virago Press, 1999

McKenna, Marthe, *I Was a Spy!*, Jarrolds Publishers, London, 1932

Morton, James, *Spies of the First World War: Under Cover for King and Kaiser*, The National Archives, 2010

Ottaway, Susan, *Violette Szabo: The Life that I Have*, Pen & Sword, 2004

Page, Gwendoline, *They Listened in Secret*, Geo. R. Reeve Ltd., 2003

Paterson, Michael, *Voices of the Code Breakers: Personal Accounts of the Secret Heroes of World War II*, David & Charles, 2007

Proctor, Tammy M., *Female Intelligence: Women and Espionage in the First World War*, New York University Press, 2003

Rimington, Stella, *Open Secret*, Arrow Books, 2002

Wheelwright, Julie, *The Fatal Lover: Mata Hari and the Myth of Women in Espionage*, Collins & Brown Ltd, 1992

Zimmeck, Meta, 'Jobs for the Girls: The Expansion of Clerical Work for Women, 1850-1914', included in *Unequal Opportunities: Women's Employment in England 1880-1918*, edited Angela V. John, Basil Blackwell Ltd., 1986

Places of interest:
Imperial War Museum, Lambeth Road, London SE1 6HZ
Has permanent exhibition: The Secret War
http://london.iwm.org.uk

The National Archives
Kew, Richmond, Surrey TW9 4DU
www.nationalarchives.gov.uk

Bletchley Park Museum,
Bletchley, Milton Keynes MK3 6EB
www.bletchleypark.org.uk

The Violette Szabo Museum
Wormelow, Herefordshire HR2 8HN
www.violette-szabo-museum.co.uk

Index